D1604505

CLASSIC
FORD TRUCKS

BY THE EDITORS OF ✖ ConsumerGuide®

Publications International, Ltd.

Louis Weber, CEO
Publications International, Ltd.
7373 North Cicero Avenue
Lincolnwood, Illinois 60712

Permission is never granted for commercial purposes.

ISBN-13: 978-1-4508-7662-9
ISBN-10: 1-4508-7662-5

Manufactured in China.

8 7 6 5 4 3 2 1

Library of Congress Control Number: 2013939310

Credits

Photography:

The editors would like to thank the following people and organizations for supplying the photography that made this book possible. They are listed below, along with the page number(s) of their photos.

Les Bidrawn: 16; **Jim Frenak:** 81; **Thomas Glatch:** 52, 97, 106, 107; **Sam Griffith:** 58, 61; **Milton Kieft:** 27, 54–55; **Dan Lyons:** 46, 64; **Vince Manocchi:** 17, 44, 46, 49, 50, 51, 57, 58, 60, 67, 74, 80, 83, 86–87, 92, 94, 95, 101, 114; **Doug Mitchel:** contents, 45, 47, 62, 65, 70–71, 123; **Mike Mueller:** 98; **Nina Padgett:** 78; **David Temple:** end sheets, 84, 124; **W. C. Waymack:** 38–39, 48, 53, 79, 110, 116.

Front Cover: Vince Manocchi

Owners:

Special thanks to the owners of the trucks featured in this book for their cooperation. Their names and page number(s) for their vehicles follow.

Henry Alvarez/HSI Motors: 98; **Ken Anderson:** 101; **Richard W. Andrews:** 46; **Robert Babcock:** 64; **John Roger Battistone:** 60; **Karl Benefiel:** 57; **Glen Bohannan:** 83; **Howard Bonner:** 45; **Brad Boyajian:** 51; **Robert Denver Brewer:** 48; **W. Parker Browne:** 27; **Dale and Ann Callen:** 94; **James R. Campbell:** 46; **Castle Amusement Park:** 17; **Kenneth A. Coppock:** 81; **Dr. Edward and Joanne Dauer:** 51; **Dells Auto Museum:** 52; **Lloyd Duzell:** 61; **James Enders:** 49; **Finn Fahey:** 110; **Ernest and Sheri Foster:** 65; **Harry Fryer:** 80; **Nelson D. Hansen:** 62; **Bill Henricks:** 53; **A. W. Higginbotham:** 124; **Kenneth M. Hustvet:** 106, 107; **Sheldon Lake:** 47; **Tom Lerdahl:** 97; **H. M. Martins:** front cover, 95; **Mark Mendelsohn:** 58; **Don Morris:** 78; **Donald F. Parker:** 50; **Jeff Pendleton:** 84; **Richard Perez:** 86–87; **Robert A. Pitts:** contents; **Dick Pyle:** 58; **Jim Reilly:** 123; **Carl M. Riggins:** 16; **Stephen Salazar:** 44; **Leroy Schaefer:** 38–39; **Robert N. Seiple:** 54–55; **Ron Shore:** end sheets; **Jerry C. Spear:** 92; **Richard Staley:** 74; **Jim Stewart:** 70–71; **Peter Strohbehn:** 110; **J. Talarico:** 93; **Dick Tait:** 67; **Greg Ueatch:** 116; **Richard L. Youngman:** 79

Our appreciation to the historical archives and media services groups at Ford Motor Company.

About The Editors of Consumer Guide®:

For more than 40 years, Consumer Guide® has been a trusted provider of new-car buying information.

The Consumer Guide® staff drives and evaluates more than 200 vehicles annually.

Consumerguide.com is one of the Web's most popular automotive resources, visited by roughly three million shoppers monthly.

The Editors of Consumer Guide® also publish the award-winning bimonthly *Collectible Automobile®* magazine.

CONTENTS

FOREWORD

To build trucks was not Henry Ford's first inclination.

He wanted to establish himself first as a maker of automobiles. His initial attempt, the 1896 Quadricycle, predated even the Ford Motor Company, and by the time of Ford's incorporation in 1903, Henry had built a selection of variably successful passenger cars and racers.

Ford made a decisive mark on the automotive arts with the Model T of 1909, a wildly popular passenger car. But things have a way of naturally evolving, and in 1917 Ford Motor introduced the Model TT-based One Ton truck chassis. Suitable for light-duty hauling, the One Ton excited some public interest and put Henry's company in the truck business to stay.

Aftermarket firms bodied those first trucks, but by 1925 Ford offered the Model T Runabout with its own factory-made Pickup body. Nearly 34,000 were sold. Closed-cab trucks soon followed.

The line expanded during the Thirties and Forties to encompass heavy-duty construction rigs, over-the-highway haulers, and a variety of trucks—many of them Cab-Over-Engine—designed for local urban duty.

The 1948 introduction of the light-duty F-1 was the beginning of the evolution of Ford trucking into what we know today. The F-1 had numerous commercial applications, but more importantly it had *personal* applications. Here at last was a typically rugged Ford truck that would appear as much at home in your driveway as in a commercial garage.

Over the decades, Ford engineers came up with larger and more diverse engines, improved wiring, stronger frames, and, for heavy-duty trucks, new automatic transmissions. Tandem rear axles helped handle increasingly big loads, and buyers got power steering, bigger brakes, aerodynamic cabs, improved creature comforts, and more.

The truck unit was busy.

Ford sold its heavy-duty-truck operation to Freightliner in 1996 in order to concentrate on the hugely popular light-truck market—and that brings us back around to the F-1, which evolved into the F-100 and was eventually superseded by the hugely popular F-150.

Ford's flagship truck still rolls to glory today, along with Explorer, Expedition, Flex, and other trucks and truck-based crossover vehicles. These very popular light trucks perpetuate the company's well-deserved reputation for ruggedness and practicality.

An ad campaign that began in 1979 still says it all: "Built Ford Tough."

①

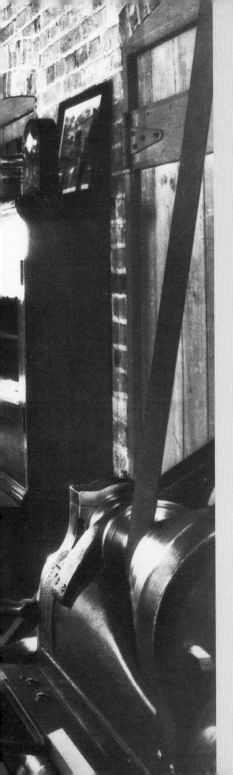

CHAPTER 1

1896—1916

What would eventually become one of the world's largest and most-respected automobile and truck manufacturers has its origins in 1896, when 33-year-old Henry Ford built his "Quadricycle," a self-propelled, carriage-like vehicle that the driver controlled with a simple tiller. Henry followed the Quadricycle with racers, light trucks, and additional "consumer" cars.

1. This reproduction at Dearborn, Michigan's Greenfield Village suggests the Bagley Avenue shed where Henry Ford constructed his first automobile, in 1896.

On June 16, 1903, Henry Ford and associates founded the Ford Motor Company. Soon thereafter, the firm began production of its first car, the two-cylinder Model A. In 1904, three more cars joined the Ford lineup: the two-cylinder Model B and Model C, and the four-cylinder Model F. By the end of the year, more than 2000 Fords had been built.

Because of booming car sales, Henry had little incentive to get into the commercial market. However, he did make a few attempts to produce specialty vehicles during the early part of the century. The first arrived in 1905. It was based on the Model C and was called the Ford Delivery Car. At $950, it was pricey and attracted few buyers.

Ford tried the commercial market again in 1907 with the Ford Delivery Van, a quasi-truck based on the four-cylinder Model N that had been introduced in '06. The idea was valid, but price militated against the Delivery Van's success. Production ended after just a year, with only about a dozen produced.

Henry Ford wasn't the sort to be bothered by the failure of a modest product in which he had little interest in the first place. At this point in his life, he invariably looked ahead—and he was looking at the car that would change everything about American motoring. He was looking at the Model T.

It was introduced in the fall of 1908 as an $825 1909 model. Although clearly based on the Model N, and thus not revolutionary as a machine, the Model T nevertheless struck a chord with buyers who appreciated the simple, reliable design, range of body styles, and seating for two or five. In order to ensure the T's success, Henry discontinued all other models, allowing for healthy production of the T.

William C. Durant established General Motors in 1908 and gave Henry some marketplace competition. In time, General Motors would become Ford Motor's chief rival, but for the moment, Ford was the undisputed industry leader. The company outgrew its Piquette Avenue (Detroit) plant in 1910 and transferred its manufacturing to a much larger facility in suburban Highland Park. Within a few years, Ford opened plants in Kansas City, Missouri; Long Island City, New York; and Minneapolis, Minnesota.

Ford returned to the commercial market in 1912 with a pair of light-duty vehicles. One was the Commercial Roadster, which was essentially a Model T Runabout with a removable rumble seat that could be replaced with a commercial body sourced by an aftermarket manufacturer.

The other commercial hauler was also car-based: the Model T Delivery Car. It was more popular than any such Ford vehicle to date, but not in the numbers needed to convince Henry to commit himself to the segment; the T Delivery Car was allowed to fade away.

In 1913, Henry and his engineers created a *moving* assembly line, a brilliant notion that reduced costs, increased worker efficiency, and hot-footed production. It was precisely the innovation Ford needed to keep manufacturing costs in check as well as satisfy increasing public demand.

Henry shocked the auto industry—and the general business-manufacturing landscape—in 1914, when he introduced a standard wage of $5 a day. This was more than double the industry's normal rate of pay and gave Ford's workers the financial wherewithal to purchase the cars they were building. With that, Ford helped to create the working-class middle class.

Late in 1915, Ford Motor Company produced its one-millionth vehicle. This milestone was celebrated almost simultaneously with the opening of another nine new assembly plants, with three more added the following year. So rapid was this expansion that Ford built its two-millionth vehicle just 18 months after reaching the one-million milestone.

This success gave Henry Ford a more sanguine attitude about his company's future. His potential product line seemed limitless, so he prepared himself to make his first committed foray into truck manufacture.

1. After building his Quadricycle, Henry did his first, secret, road test in the rainy wee hours of June 4, 1896. He continued to test the automobile in and around Detroit, often seeking out the worst roads to determine the Quadricycle's capabilities.

2. Henry Ford's first automobile was powered by a water-cooled, four-stroke, two-cylinder engine that developed about four horsepower. Top speed approached 20 mph. Steering was done by tiller.

SOROSIS
ALL STYLES $3.50
THE NEW SHOE FOR WOMEN
STANDARD OF THE WORLD.

Newcomb, Endicott & Co.

1

1. Before the turn of the 20th century, Henry Ford's Detroit Automobile Company, a precursor to Ford Motor, announced plans to build a delivery van. At least one had been built by 1900. Tiller steering continued; tires were solid rubber.

2. Detroit's McMichael photo studio snapped this early study of young Henry Ford. In just a few years, Henry would help transform the entire city.

3. Ford's Mack Avenue factory (shown) produced the predecessor of the Model T, the Model N. Subsequent T development and production happened at Ford's Piquette Avenue plant.

1. Storage baskets, as on this 1903 Model A, were common accessories for early Model T Fords. The T Runabout sold for $825 while the four-seat tonneau went for $850.

2. Ford's Delivery Car was introduced in 1905 and rode a Model C chassis. The Delivery was Ford Motor's first attempt at a cargo vehicle. Only a handful were built before the body style was discontinued. The later example seen here rides a 1912 Model T chassis.

①

2

1. This promotional photo highlights the "Watch the Fords Go By" slogan, which was introduced in 1907. The phrase became very well known, not least because it adorned the sides of trains carrying Ford product

2. Ford service and sales branches needed light trucks with which to do customer calls. The 1913 Model T Runabout seen here was not a factory-built truck. That would come later. For the time being, pickup boxes were farmed out to aftermarket manufacturers.

3. Depot Hacks, like this one on a 1914 Model T chassis, were forerunners of station wagons, equally at home with suitcases and other light cargo as with passengers. The bodies were built for Ford by outside suppliers.

4. In warm, dry weather, a 1914 Depot Hack offered pleasant motoring between train station and hotel. Wet weather was another issue altogether, so even though the Hack was practical, it probably was not beloved.

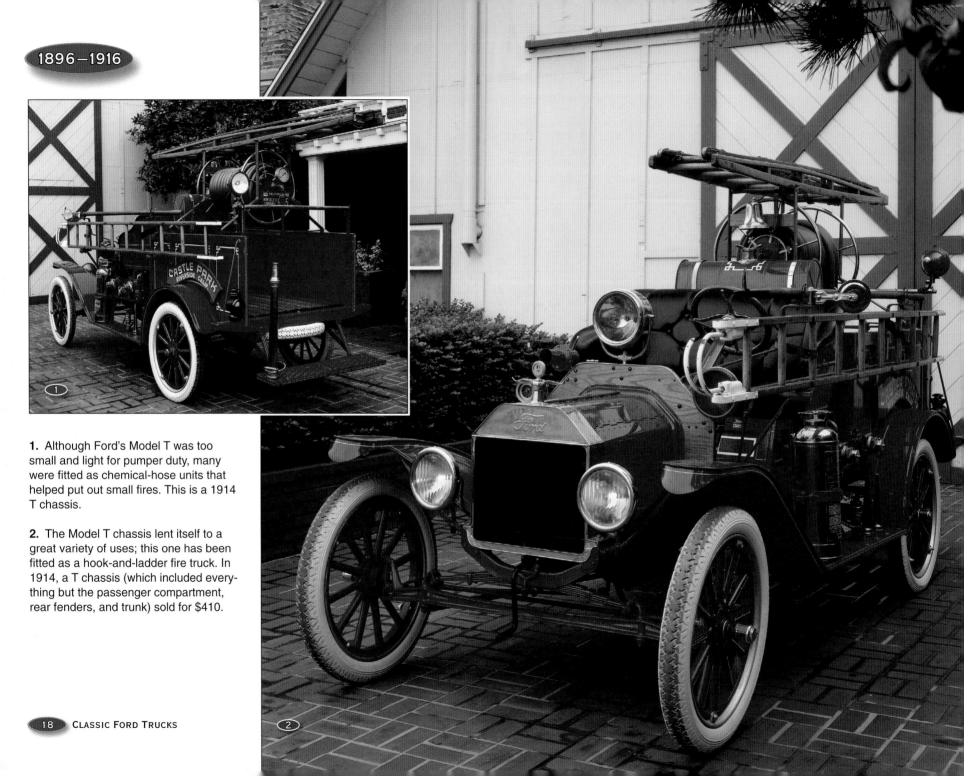

1. Although Ford's Model T was too small and light for pumper duty, many were fitted as chemical-hose units that helped put out small fires. This is a 1914 T chassis.

2. The Model T chassis lent itself to a great variety of uses; this one has been fitted as a hook-and-ladder fire truck. In 1914, a T chassis (which included every-thing but the passenger compartment, rear fenders, and trunk) sold for $410.

3. A former farmhand, Henry Ford continued to enjoy farmlike labor after becoming an auto mogul. He's seen here chopping firewood sometime in 1916.

4. Henry Ford had a keen interest in agriculture—hence this Model T-based tractor with bent frame rails that allowed high ground clearance. Load stress on a tractor engine called for additional cooling, which was provided by a hood-mounted water tank (shown). The other tank contained fuel.

CHAPTER 2

1917–1924

After observing his Model Ts being turned into light trucks for several years, Henry Ford finally decided he wanted to manufacture a proper Ford truck. On July 27, 1917, he entered the truck business with a new chassis: the Model TT, which was rated for one ton. Now a customer could buy a stripped Model T chassis for light duty or a heavier-duty Model TT variant for bigger jobs. The uprated frame put Ford in the truck business—for good.

1. This paddy wagon had mesh sides and parallel bench seating. The solid-rubber tires were ventilated at the sidewalls to allow flex that made the ride less harsh.

1

P.D. 279

POLICE DEPARTMENT.

Nineteen seventeen brought two other events critical to the company's future success: the introduction of the Fordson tractor, and the birth of Henry Ford's grandson, Henry Ford II, who was the son of Henry's only child, Edsel.

In 1918, 25-year-old Edsel assumed the presidency of the Ford Motor Company, establishing a modicum of control but laboring beneath the watchful eye of his father. With American involvement in the Great War (World War I), Ford produced war materiel for the first time. Model T ambulances had been shipped to France since 1917, and the company opened a dedicated plant to manufacture submarine-chasing Eagle boats.

The war ended on November 11, 1918. War contracts had helped the company's financials, and Ford was quick to return to peacetime production. The three-millionth Model T was assembled in 1919, the year that Edsel Ford's second son, Benson, was born. Most important was the beginning of construction on the River Rouge manufacturing complex, which would eventually grow into a self-contained megafactory. Even without River Rouge, Ford Motor produced nearly half of all vehicles sold in the United States in 1919.

By 1920, custom-bodied commercial Fords were common sights. Second only to the touring car in sales, Ford's unfinished truck chassis were fitted for duty in countless ways. Priced at $640, the Model TT trucks typically left the factory as little more than cabs atop bare chassis. Anxious that they might be left behind, many former carriage builders found new life finishing Ford trucks for specific duty. Special bodies served a variety of needs, such as panel-side and open-side deliveries, tankers, and pickup-style "expresses." Cab styles also varied, from little more than a suspended wood roof to full enclosures.

Nineteen twenty-one brought mixed results for Ford. In May, the company celebrated production of its 5-millionth Model T, but the good news was offset by the defection of Ford's brilliant production boss, William Knudsen, to Chevrolet. It was largely because of this that Chevrolet became an automotive juggernaut, passing Ford on the sales charts by the end of the decade. The irony is that Knudsen was virtually driven from Ford by Henry, who frequently countermanded Knudsen's orders and who precipitated the break by assigning responsibility for Ford's European operations to son Edsel rather than to Knudsen.

Another piece of negative news for 1921 was that Dodge Brothers, Inc., an up-and-coming rival, signed an agreement with the Graham Brothers Truck Company to become the sole distributor of that brand. Later in the decade, Dodge would absorb Graham and become another serious competitor to Ford.

In 1922, Ford delivered more than 150,000 Model TT chassis. Truck prices for 1923 started at $380, down $65 from the previous year. Ford trucks enjoyed the same styling enhancements as the rest of the Model T line, such as higher fenders and wider running boards.

In February 1922, Ford purchased the assets of the Lincoln Motor Company for $8 million.

Things looked even better in '23, as a new blast furnace was dedicated at the River Rouge Complex and production of the Fordson tractor at that facility set records.

For 1923, Ford updated the look of the Model T cars and Model TT trucks. Production of all vehicles topped 1.8 million units for the year.

An emphatic 1923 print ad shouted "CUT YOUR COSTS! Buy a Ford." The suggestion would have had special meaning for operators of commercial truck fleets.

Finally, after watching other firms make money with truck-chassis conversions, Henry Ford made an important decision...

1. The United States entered the Great War (later called World War I) in April 1917. Ford Motor manufactured thousands of ambulances for the effort.

FORD MODEL T ONE TON TRUCK

This is the Model T One Ton Truck just as we deliver to the purchaser, without body. The equipment includes hood for motor, front fenders, stepping boards, two side lights, two head lights, one tail light, horn and set of tools. All Ford cars sold f.o.b. Detroit

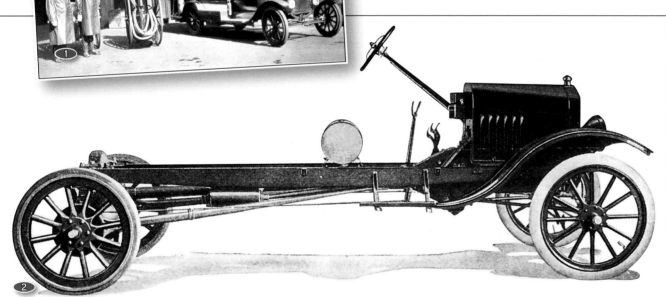

22387-6-14-18

1. Ford's first one-ton chassis was priced at $600, making it an appealing buy for municipalities. This 1919 fire truck put a Runabout body on the chassis but dispensed with doors, windshield, and folding top.

2. The new TT chassis had a longer, strengthened Model T frame, stouter rear springs, solid-rubber tires at the rear, and a worm-drive rear axle. The first one rolled off the line on July 27, 1917.

3. By 1918, Ford was building dedicated truck chassis. A one-ton unit listed for $600 in '18, significantly more than a standard Model T chassis, which cost just $325. This truck has a stake-bed body and a canopied passenger compartment.

4. Oakland, California-based Dreyer's Grand Ice Cream used this 1920 Model T truck to make deliveries. Like Ford, Dreyer's still prospers today.

5. This Model T, from around 1918, was fitted with a cargo box for factory use. For consumers, outside firms continued to supply the boxes.

1. Following conversion from Model T to a truck, this truck was converted to a snow cat. A second rear axle allowed use of tanklike treads.

2. This 1920 Depot Hack has rolled-up canvas side curtains and Ford's demountable rims, which allowed for easier repair of flats. The outer rim that held the tire could be separated from the wheel hub, which remained on the vehicle.

3. U.S. business and finance were rolling right along in 1923, so a stern-faced cartoon spokesman who extolled Ford product seemed persuasive. The poster was issued in cooperation with the Akron (Ohio) Tire Display Company.

4. Modest alterations that included a cargo bed made this 1922 Model T-based light truck suitable for light fire duty.

④

CLASSIC FORD TRUCKS 27

1. Monroe, Michigan's Jones Transfer Co. went to the aftermarket to create the closed-cab, stake-body truck seen here. And after 1920, some fenders left the factory in colors other than black.

2. This Model T-based passenger vehicle has wood-paneled bodysides and a side-mounted spare fitted to a demountable rim.

②

2

3

1. For 1924, the Model T was given a taller radiator and hood, as seen on this panel-bodied example that was owned by Detroit's Pioneer Tea Company. Increasingly, trucks were expected to traverse awful roads.

2. Lighter Model T chassis were still available for light-duty hauling. Note the oval fuel tank that was fitted to Model Ts beginning in the early Twenties.

3. Ford's first truck cab appeared in 1924. It was called the Open Cab and had a slanted windshield and C-shaped side openings. This one was fitted to a Model TT one-ton chassis.

1. The Express Body pickup bed was new for 1924, and was Ford's first truck bed of any kind. This one, riding a Model TT Open Cab chassis, has a canopy top, screens, and side curtains.

2. By the early Twenties, many aftermarket manufacturers produced accessories needed to customize a Model T chassis to the buyer's specific needs. This closed florist's van has sliding-door entry and a "Biflex" bumper.

②

1. Another Model-TT chassis Express Body, meaning a pickup bed.

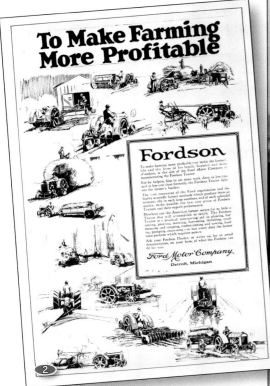

2. Many farmers of the mid-Twenties still used horses for plowing, so a great many Fordson tractor ads made a point of emphasizing the machine's useful versatility.

3. Henry Ford and son Edsel, with a Fordson tractor. With the Fordson line, Henry created tractors that were within the financial means of most professional farmers.

1. A long leather belt connected the pulley of this Fordson tractor to a threshing machine. Tractors were used as stationary power sources nearly as often as they were for plowing and other mobile duties.

2. A Fordson fitted with wooden skis and enormous crawler tracks hauled this load of timber in the mid-Twenties.

3. A farmer poses proudly with his well-used 1915 or '16 Model T pickup and his Fordson tractor.

CHAPTER 3
1925—1937

By 1925, the American automobile industry was a fixture of daily life and a key part of the national economy. Individual automakers would prosper or perish, but for the industry in general, the only direction was up. Commercial vehicles promised to be an enormous market segment.

1. Two-tone Vermilion Red & Black highlights this 1930 Model A pickup in Deluxe trim, with stainless-steel radiator and headlights, wide whitewalls, and a chromed spare tire cover.

1

Having become a dominant manufacturer and marketer of personal cars, Ford built on the success of its one-ton truck chassis of 1917 when it introduced the Model T Runabout with optional pickup body in 1925. The result was a light-duty truck based on a car chassis—and thus "familiar" to car buyers. In other words, you could buy a truck without feeling as if you were buying a truck. As the baby brother to Ford's Model TT with Express (pickup) body, the Runabout sold for just $281. That may seem like a giveaway price, but Ford Motor could afford it, selling cars during 1925 as quickly as it could build them and opening its first plant in Mexico. The company built its 12-millionth vehicle that year and set a new truck production record of more than 270,000 units. And William Clay Ford, Henry's third grandson, was born.

In order to stimulate sales of the now old-fashioned Model T, 1926 brought body colors other than black: gray, green, and maroon. But the writing was on the wall. The Model T still sold well, but cars from Chevrolet and other makers had superseded it; its days were numbered. Shortly after building the 15-millionth copy in 1927, Ford brought all production to a halt.

The shutdown was strictly temporary, as Ford had an all-new design waiting to make its debut. And indeed, what rolled out of Ford plants later that year would make buyers forget all about the old Tin Lizzie.

The new Ford was called the Model A, and it was introduced to the public on December 2, 1927. The Model AA truck line soon followed, and both were immediate hits with buyers. More stylish than the Model Ts and TTs that they replaced, the new cars and trucks came with more standard equipment, a more powerful engine, and an easier-to-use transmission. So advanced and price-competitive were these Fords that they became the hits of the 1928 model year.

Ford trumped the industry again in 1929 when it introduced a new, factory-built, light-duty model, the wood-bodied Station Wagon, a follow-on to the earlier, simply canopied Depot Hack.

New models from Ford or any other manufacturer paled next to the events of Black Tuesday—October 29, 1929—the first day of what became a calamitous stock market crash that ultimately plunged America into economic Depression. For much of the decade that followed, many Americans could barely buy food, let alone a new car or truck. Many automakers went under.

Styling changes to the 1930 and '31 Model A cars and Model AA trucks widened the models' appeal, but Ford pulled a major coup in 1932 when its familiar four-cylinder engine was joined by a V-8—a move that trumped Chevrolet's heretofore segment-leading six. The V-8, installed in what Ford called the Model 18, was an immediate and tremendous success. A less-expensive four, running in the Model B, also was offered. But most buyers selected the eight, and the four faded away after 1934.

Nineteen thirty-three was Ford Motor's 30th Anniversary, and it saw production of the company's 21-millionth vehicle. Ford was a major participant in Chicago's Century of Progress International Exposition, and in Dearborn, Henry Ford opened his Greenfield Village complex, a tribute to a vanished way of life that had nurtured Henry as a child and as a very young man.

Open-cab Ford trucks were history by 1935, when Ford cars and trucks received significant styling and engineering upgrades that attracted buyers.

A forward-control chassis introduced in 1937 put Ford in the transit-bus business because the new technology allowed the bus's driver to sit alongside the engine rather than behind it. The company also began to offer trucks in uplevel Deluxe trim.

Because Ford had discontinued its four, in 1937 the company offered an "economy" 136-cid V-8 developing 60 horsepower—a considerably more frugal engine than the 221-cid, 85-horse standard version. But the new eight wasn't powerful enough to suit buyers, and soon joined the four in Ford history books.

1. A radical restyle for 1926 gave the Model T a taller hood that flowed straight into the cowl, as seen on this Runabout.

2. A Model T Runabout with a pickup body appeared for 1925 and was Ford's first real light-duty pickup.

JAMES CARGO
WHOLESALE FRUITS·VEGETABLES
SPECIAL BANANA DELIVERY
2416 Market St. Eastern Market
Detroit, Mich. Phone Cherry 7660

1. By 1926, Ford was making its own truck bodies, but aftermarket suppliers continued to offer special-purpose varieties, such as this useful panel delivery fitted to a Model T chassis.

2. In 1928, the completely new Model A replaced the venerable Model T. The A truck chassis was termed AA and was rated at 1.5 tons. An "A" is pictured.

3. By the time Model T production ceased in 1927, more than 15 million of the cars had been built. This '27 Runabout pickup was among the last of the Ts. Although the truck is two-toned, Ford once again mandated that fenders and running boards be black.

③

1

1. A 1930 Model A Sedan Delivery in Deluxe trim shows off its side-hinged rear door.

2. A closed-cab Model A pickup. Both the A and AA models ran with a 200-cid four that produced 40 horsepower—twice that of the Model T's 177-cid four—along with a sliding-gear three-speed transmission.

3. Heavy-duty Ford trucks adopted steel disc wheels during the 1929 model year and offered dual rear wheels as optional items. This rare, restored 1930 AA dump truck is powered by a 200-cid, 40-horse four similar to the unit in contemporary Model A cars but mated to a four-speed transmission that gave a wider range of gear ratios.

4. General Electric used Deluxe Model A pickups in 1930 to promote appliance sales. This model's high-walled cargo bed was integral with the cab and was topped by chrome rails. This body style was discontinued after 1931.

1. A 1931 Model A postal truck with the utilitarian sliding side door in the open position.

2. A 1931 Model A pickup in Deluxe trim, with a box that was longer, wider, and taller than the previous version's.

3. This 1931 Deluxe Panel Body Funeral Service Car was mounted on the 131.5-inch AA chassis. Its wide side windows immediately identify it.

4. Ford introduced the Town Car Delivery for 1930. It came with carriage lamps and a bright metal spare tire cover, and could be fitted with a canopy over the driver's area. The aluminum cargo compartment was lined with wood paneling. This distinctive body style would disappear after 1931.

1. Ford's Combined Dump and Coal Body had taller sides than those on standard dump bodies. This Model AA dates from 1930.

2. At $600, the 1932 Station Wagon cost $60 more than a Fordor sedan. The advantage was seating for eight rather than for five.

3. Restoration of this 1931 Model A Special Delivery returned it to the livery and other markings of a family business.

4. This restored '34 Pickup runs with Ford's flathead V-8, an engine with popularity sufficient to encourage Ford to phase out the four during the model year.

5. This is a rare image of a prototype of the scarce '32 Model B Open Cab Pickup. Because the wheelbase had been stretched nearly three inches, to 106, compared to the Model A, Model B pickup beds grew more than 10 inches in length, to nearly 70.

6. For 1932, the flathead V-8 noted above was introduced as an alternative to the familiar four-cylinder motor. The eight (seen here) displaced 221 cubic inches and developed 65 horsepower.

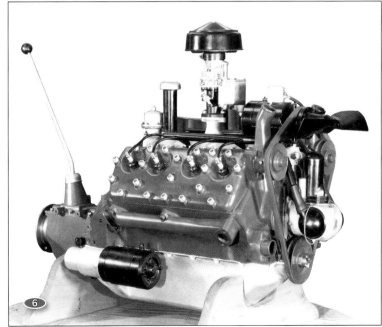

1. A restored 1934 Model BB stake bed rides the standard 131.5-inch-wheelbase chassis. This example has its original oak bed.

2. Ford sold Model BB chassis for many applications, including school bus use in 1934.

3. A 1933 BB Stake truck sported a rounded grille and an arched headlight bar. The rear leaf springs were inverted and centered over the axle in what we'd now call "normal" fashion.

4. The 7500-pound curb weight of this Texaco tanker on the 157-inch wheelbase doubled under a full load of fuel.

1. For 1936, the Sedan Delivery continued to be based on the car line. That explains the full, carlike fenders and tapered headlight housings. Note the side-hinged rear door.

2. The truck line was redesigned for 1935 and was little changed for '36 (shown). Carlike modifications included a backswept windshield and a curvaceous grille.

3. The Sedan Delivery was car-based, but the Panel Delivery (shown) was not, so it carried truck styling along with dual side-hinged rear doors, a larger load compartment, and higher payload capacity. This 1936 model is nearly identical to the redesigned '35.

4. A fuller grille and a vee'd windshield marked Ford's 1937 truck line. All pickups now had a V-8, but buyers had a choice of the established 221-cid, 85-horsepower version or a new 136-cid motor with 60 horses.

④

CHAPTER 4

1938–1947

Both 1938 and 1939 were significant years for Ford cars and trucks. Pickups were fitted with a new cab and revised front-end sheet metal and bed for '38, while light-duty versions got a new chassis. Rated at one ton, the new series was called, appropriately enough, the "One-Tonner." A Three-Quarter Tonner came on line the following year. Nineteen thirty-eight also brought a Ford innovation that was an industry first, the Cab-Over-Engine (COE) models.

1. Sedan Deliveries used Deluxe car styling for 1940, with slatted "gills" flanking a horizontal-bar grille. The new interiors had two-tone colors and chrome accents.

The 1939 introduction of a sister make, Mercury—which allowed Ford to compete in the mid-priced field against Pontiac, Oldsmobile, Hudson, and Dodge—brought with it a larger V-8 of 239 cubic inches and 95 horsepower. This engine soon found its way into Ford trucks.

Henry Ford, at 75, finally bowed to buyer and internal corporate pressure and replaced his vehicles' old-fashioned mechanically actuated brakes with modern hydraulic units. Virtually all of Ford's competitors had made the switch years before, and though Henry didn't trust the new technology, its absence on Ford product was considered an easily avoided safety detriment.

As the Thirties concluded, Canada joined Great Britain in the late summer of '39 to declare war on the aggressor nation of Germany. Soon thereafter, the Ford Motor Company of Canada, Ltd. undertook production of military-specification vehicles for the war effort. By 1941, Ford began producing a version of the 4×4 "jeep" universal vehicle for the military, and also started constructing new war-related plants—just in case the USA got drawn into the conflict.

Within weeks of Japan's December 7 attack on the U.S. naval base at Pearl Harbor, Hawaii, Ford suspended civilian production to concentrate on building B-24 Liberator bombers, aircraft engines, tanks, jeeps, wood gliders, and military versions of 1942 cars, pickups, and heavy-duty trucks. Naturally, all of this contributed to Ford's expertise in truck manufacture.

A new six-cylinder engine was introduced for 1941 to complement Ford's flathead V-8. The six had more torque than the eight and provided somewhat better fuel economy. During this same period, some light- and medium-duty trucks could be had with a four-cylinder motor based on the one that powered Ford's tractors.

As the need for military vehicles began to wane late in 1944, the government allowed Ford to resume limited production of heavy-duty trucks for civilian use, and still more early in 1945. An improved V-8 engine was one result, as well as reworked cabs with a one-piece cowl, top, roof, and windshield-pillar stamping. They also got a new instrument panel and sealed-beam headlights.

Henry Ford's only son, and FoMoCo's president, Edsel, died prematurely in 1943. Henry again took over day-to-day executive duties at the company but, at 80, was unable to function effectively. Because Ford Motor was essential to the U.S. war effort, the federal government selected a successor, Henry's grandson, Henry II, who was completing a Navy stint as he prepared to step into Ford's top job. The transition happened in September 1945, and Henry II used the time to establish his preeminence. He fired Harry Bennett, the elder Henry's coarse, longtime labor "enforcer," and installed a brilliant older executive, Ernest Breech, as his mentor.

Henry II inherited a company that had been on unsteady financial footing before the war, and that emerged from the war in hardly better shape. In these early months, Henry II would be severely tested. But he was blessed with an analytical mind and a willingness to listen to and take the counsel of others. At the same time, he was a risk-taker with a useful product sense.

Ford's Cab-Over-Engine trucks returned to the lineup in 1946 and were joined by some heavier-duty two-ton models. These "Ford Heavies" had reinforced frames, two-speed rear axles, heavier-duty springs, and larger tires.

On April 17, 1947, the company and the nation mourned the loss of one of the industry's great pioneers, when Henry Ford passed away at his home. He was 83.

1. For 1938, Ford pickups got bulbous front and rear fenders and a new oval grille. The cab and pickup bed were also new.

CALIFORNIA
1V79517

1-2. This restored wrecker has the distinctive Cab-Over-Engine (COE) setup that was introduced for 1938. The configuration provided all the pulling power of standard models but with considerably less overall length.

3. Although the body was new, truck styling continued to dominate Panel Delivery models of 1938.

4. This 1938 fire truck saw duty at Ford's River Rouge manufacturing complex. The pumper handled blazes that did not require help from municipal fire departments, or that could be held in check until outside help could arrive.

5. This 1939 Cab-Over-Engine (COE) Stake Bed delivered soft drinks and mixers. Because so many customers for such items were located on busy city streets, the COE design allowed for trucks with full cargo capacities, but of sufficiently short overall length to help ensure maneuverability in tight spaces.

1. Another veteran of Ford's River Rouge plant, this 1939 fire truck later saw duty with the Flint, Michigan, fire department. Note the wide-open cab.

2. Model-year 1940 marked the first time since 1932 that Ford pickups shared current Ford-car styling. That meant a vee'd grille, pointed hood, and headlights that were faired into the fenders.

1. Cargo from a Navy ship is unloaded onto a 1941 COE Flatbed. The previous upright-oval grille has been replaced by a more carlike design.

2. Restored to reflect its past life as a Bell System vehicle, this '40 Pickup has a custom utility box that is at once convenient and not easily tampered with.

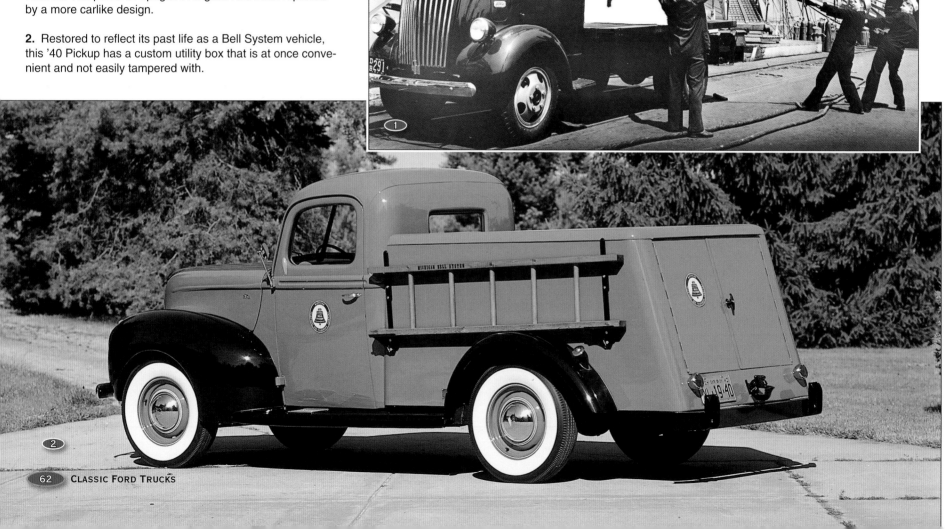

③

3. Ford tractor-trailer rigs dated back to the Twenties, and by 1941 the cabs were powerful enough to tow heavily loaded trailers. Note that this setup is a heavy-hauling dualie with tandem trailers.

4. Cloverland Dairy used a shortened Ford one-ton chassis and a custom delivery body to make milk deliveries in 1941. Trucks intended for this kind of local work were often ordered with Ford's economical new four-cylinder tractor engine.

④

1938–1947

1. In 1941, "the ice man" delivered to homes as well as to businesses. The Dunham Pure Ice Company of Baton Rouge, Louisiana, operated this truck shortly before America's entry into World War II.

2. This restored 1941 Pickup has been in the owner's family since the vehicle was new. The '41s are widely considered among the most handsome Ford Pickup models ever built.

3. Because civilian vehicle production ended on February 10, 1942, Ford was able to turn out only a small number of freshly styled 1942 trucks.

③

1. Even before America's formal entry into the war, Ford and other automakers were engaged in the manufacture of war materiel. Ford built several prototype ¾-ton military trucks, including this forward-control four-wheel-drive cargo job.

2. At the same time that Ford cars and trucks used the firm's well-worn cast-iron flathead V-8, Ford-built tanks were powered by advanced 1100-cubic-inch, double-overhead-cam aluminum-block V-8s.

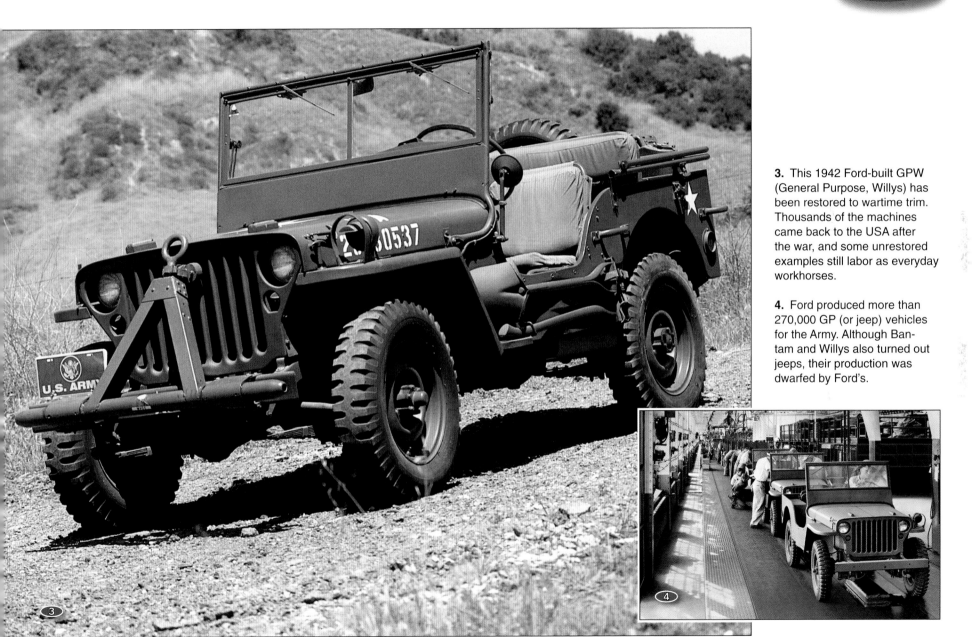

3. This 1942 Ford-built GPW (General Purpose, Willys) has been restored to wartime trim. Thousands of the machines came back to the USA after the war, and some unrestored examples still labor as everyday workhorses.

4. Ford produced more than 270,000 GP (or jeep) vehicles for the Army. Although Bantam and Willys also turned out jeeps, their production was dwarfed by Ford's.

1. Ford's styling and engineering departments envisioned postwar trucks that were little changed from their wartime cousins. However, the 221-cid flathead V-8 that had powered Fords since 1932 was retired for 1946 and replaced with a 239-cid Mercury unit.

2. Ford cars for 1946 were merely warmed-over and look very much like this '42. Carlike cues are very apparent on this Sedan Delivery.

3. In a fanciful bit of marketing, New Era potato chips linked itself with health and a youthful, shapely figure. Vehicles like this 1946 one-ton truck were now referred to at the factory as "Tonners."

4. Materials were still in short supply immediately after the war, which is why this 1946 Panel Delivery sports a spare tire that's a wheel only—no rubber! As you might expect, truck companies did not have sudden access to a wealth of new tires at war's end. To the contrary, they had to operate with vehicles designed to be as easy on rubber as possible.

CHAPTER 5

1948–1952

A new era began at the Ford Motor Company in January 1948 with the release of an all-new line of trucks that Ford called the F-Series. Ford promoted the series as its "Bonus Built Line" that covered a wide range of models with different cab and chassis combinations. In fact, add them all up and buyers were looking at more than 100 combinations of chassis, body, and cab.

1. Ford's F-Series of light pickups set Ford up in a market segment it still dominates today. This '51 F-1 is identified by a newly toothy grille and a fresh hood badge. Pickup beds now had wood floors rather than steel, plus larger rear windows than before.

If all of this sounds aggressively proactive—it wasn't. To the contrary, Ford had been scooped a year earlier, when Chevy's "Advance Design" pickups were the first wholly redesigned light-duty trucks from any of the Big Three. Until that line was retired in 1955, the Advance Design trucks were the best sellers of their class.

At Ford, the foundation of the Bonus Built Line was light-duty, 1/2-ton-rated F-1 pickups; in stepped fashion, choices ran all the way to the Extra Heavy-Duty, three-ton-rated F-8. (Before 1948, the top-rated Fords were Two Tonners.) All of these trucks came with completely redesigned cabs and all-new front-end sheet metal. The corporation spent more than a million dollars to improve the aptly named Million-Dollar Cabs, with owners getting more useful placement of controls and gauges, as well as improved room and comfort.

In a departure from previous practice, conventional and Cab-Over-Engine Ford trucks shared the same cab.

A year later, the vision of Henry II was reflected in the all-new '49 car line, which brought integrated fenders and sleek, slab-sided styling. The redesign was an immediate hit, but because it made no provision for a Sedan Delivery model, the truck line wasn't affected for the 1949 model year. What the truck line did get, however, were a couple of new stand-up Parcel Delivery vehicles.

Although Ford trucks would be undeniably flashy by the end of the Fifties, those that ushered in the decade could only be described as subdued and little-changed from 1949. Aside from a larger "Big Six" engine for F-6 buyers who didn't want the V-8, there wasn't much new or exciting for dealers to trumpet.

Not so for 1951, which brought the first F-Series restyle since that line's 1948 debut.

F-Series conventionals and C-Series COE trucks got modified front fenders, grille cavity, and grille. Hoods and cabs were changed as well, along with dashboards and new, substantially larger rear windows.

Also available for '51—and for the first time since the late Thirties—were two levels of cab trim, the standard Five Star Cab and the deluxe Five Star Extra. The latter had such niceties as foam seat padding, extra sound-deadening material, bright metal trim around the windshield and vent windows, plus argent-finished grille bar, locks and armrests on both doors, two-toned upholstery, a dome light, and twin horns.

In a '51 booklet called *Ford Truck Economy Run,* customers offered testimonials to the dollar sense of their Ford trucks, from F-1 all the way up to the big F-8 models. Ford said the booklet's conclusions were based on a survey of some 5500 buyers of earlier Ford trucks.

New overhead-valve engines were introduced for 1952, but not all of them made it to the truck line—at least, not yet. The first new overhead-valve motor, a six-cylinder displacing 215 cubic inches, was available in Ford trucks from the F-1 through the F-5, as well as in Ford cars. The engine produced 101 horsepower at 3500 rpm with a compression ratio of 7.0:1. Still on the economy kick, Ford called the engine the "Cost Clipper Six."

The other ohv motor was a large V-8 based on a new Lincoln engine that was offered as a Y-block "Cargo King" 279 and a larger Cargo King 317. It was available with the big F-7 and F-8 models only; smaller trucks came standard with the old flathead V-8.

Bonus Built meant plenty of bread and butter for Ford, but something even fresher was right around the corner.

1. Model-year 1948 was momentous at Ford Truck, as it introduced a new ½-ton light truck called the F-1. Rear fenders were styled to match the profile of the fronts. More importantly, Ford virtually created a whole new market segment and made it its own.

THE LAND OF ENCHANTMENT
1 ⚜ 2798 TRUCK
NEW MEXICO

1948–1952

1. The squared-off front fenders of the 1948 F-1 wrapped smoothly into the front fascia, which carried a prominent horizontal-bar grille. A one-piece windshield was also new. Note the "F-1" designation just above the trailing edge of the front fender.

2. From front bumper to rear, the '48 Panel Truck was completely new—a significant accomplishment in the post-war marketplace. The Panel's cargo volume increased, as did the size of the rear access doors.

①

②

3. Ads for Ford's heavy-duty trucks highlighted the new 337-cid flathead V-8 found in the equally new F-7 (2½-ton) and F-8 (3-ton) Extra Heavy Duty models. Horsepower was a healthy 145.

4. This 1948 1½-ton-rated F-5 chassis had a special "bottle" body.

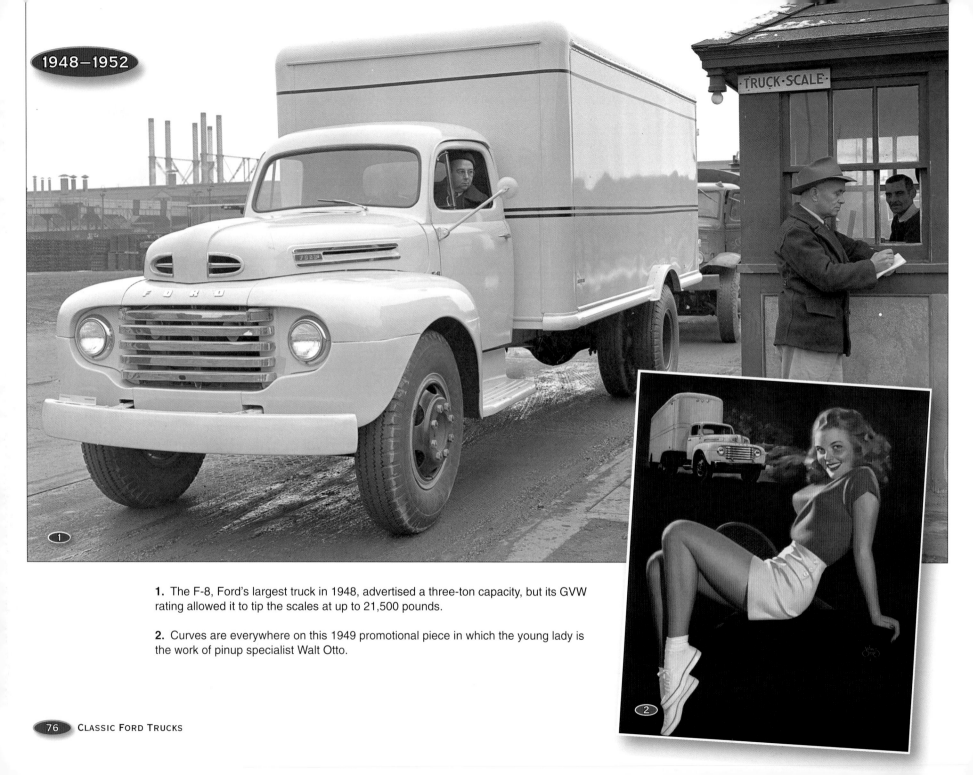

TRUCK·SCALE

1. The F-8, Ford's largest truck in 1948, advertised a three-ton capacity, but its GVW rating allowed it to tip the scales at up to 21,500 pounds.

2. Curves are everywhere on this 1949 promotional piece in which the young lady is the work of pinup specialist Walt Otto.

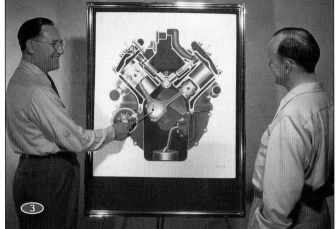

3. A cross-section illustration of Ford's V-8 shows the side-mounted valves and oddly shaped combustion chambers inherent in flathead designs.

4. Stake-bed trucks were available in conventional and Cab-Over-Engine designs for 1948; shown is a two-ton COE F-6. Whatever the cab configuration, the trucks could be powered by a 95-horsepower 226-cid six or a 100-horse 239-cid V-8.

1. Because all Ford trucks shared the same "face" of the corporate redesign, even a specialty vehicle like this '49 Parcel Delivery chassis (new that year), which began as just a front end and windshield, could easily be ID'd as a Ford. An aftermarket supplier added the body.

2-3. Good Humor Corporation of America operated a fleet of ice cream trucks nationwide, becoming so well liked that a movie comedy, *The Good Humor Man,* was a hit in 1950. Note the open cab and specialized freezer-unit body.

4. The 1949 F-1 is widely recognized for its design simplicity and purity of line. There was no badging to indicate which engine it carried.

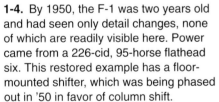

1-4. By 1950, the F-1 was two years old and had seen only detail changes, none of which are readily visible here. Power came from a 226-cid, 95-horse flathead six. This restored example has a floor-mounted shifter, which was being phased out in '50 in favor of column shift.

5. This carefully restored 1950 F-7 pumper wears a sleek body by Howe. The truck originally labored for Martin Township in Michigan.

1. Newly optional for the 1950 F-6 was a 254-cubic-inch six rated at 110 horsepower.

2. A '51 "Big Job" F-8 dualie tractor awaits its driver outside a Vernor's bottling plant. Only the F-8 and F-7 were fitted with Ford's big 336-cid flathead V-8, which was available with an exclusive five-speed transmission. The Vernor's tractor is fitted with cast wheels and demountable rims, which were newly available for 1951, and which allowed the same spare tire to be used on any wheel.

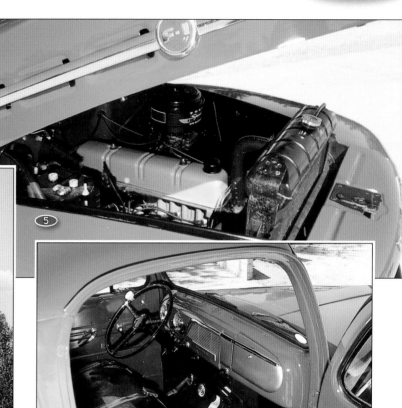

3-6. Changes to truck styling for 1952 were most noticeable to the trim on the nose and the sides of the hood. (A fresh design would come in 1953.) The big change was a new 215-cid, six-cylinder engine with overhead valves. Horsepower came in at 101.

1. A 1952 F-5 with beverage body alerts bystanders to "Drink-A-Bite to Eat." This is a 1½-ton truck that was available as a school bus chassis, COE, or a conventional, as seen here. GVW ranged from 10,000 to 14,500 pounds.

2. F-7 Big Job trucks for 1952 could be had with a new 279-cid overhead-valve V-8 rated at 145 horsepower. F-8s got an even larger and more powerful version, at 317 cid and 155 hp.

CHAPTER 6

1953—1960

Ford Motor Company celebrated its Golden Anniversary in 1953 by introducing a completely redesigned line of F-Series trucks. The company also took the opportunity to alter its model designations, changing F-1 to F-100, and so on, right up to the big new heavy-duty, the F-900.

1. At its Golden Anniversary and after, Ford continued to develop its big trucks but really made hay with its light-duty series. Ford cars and trucks alike got quad headlights for 1958, as on this F-100. Grilles were redesigned to accommodate.

"Bonus Built" was out for '53; now, the series comprised the "Economy Truck Line," in an effort to promote operational efficiencies. A new hood emblem—depicting a gear cog bisected by a lightning bolt—joined the new nomenclature. And for the first time in Ford-truck history, an automatic transmission was offered as an option, though initially on F-100s only.

The venerable flathead V-8 vanished from Ford trucks after 1953 and was replaced for '54 by the new overhead-valve V-8 that was installed in Ford cars that same year. This "Y-Block" engine displaced the same 239 cubic inches as the flathead but produced nearly 15 percent more horsepower.

Also new for '54 were available tandem rear-axle setups for heavy-duty work. The option was restricted to the T-700 and T-800 models ("T" for "tandem," of course). Ford also added a pair of heavy-duty Cab-Over-Engine models, the C-700 and C-900. And 1954 brought the expansion of the automatic transmission option to the F-250 and F-350 trucks.

A redesigned car line and the introduction of a sporty personal car called Thunderbird dominated Ford news for 1955. Changes to the truck line were minimal, with little besides a revised grille and exterior trim pieces.

Changes were more significant for '56, when Ford's trucks gained wrap-around windshields, a popular feature on cars that brought the truck line into friendlier design territory than earlier.

Rival General Motors had brought out stylish new trucks for 1955, and for two years Ford had to face that competition with a warmed-over line that dated to 1953. That made 1957 a very big year for Ford dealers, when not one but three good-looking trucks were introduced. The F-Series now had a completely fresh look, more square than before, as well as wider cabs, hidden running boards, flush-mounted front fenders, and a full-width hood.

The year also brought a choice of two pickup beds, the traditional Flareside, with a narrow bed and attached rear fenders; and the new Styleside, with straight-through fenders. A straight-sided bed was nothing new to the industry, but unlike other manufacturers, Ford offered its Styleside pickup box at no extra charge.

Significant, too, was the new car-truck hybrid called Ranchero. Based on a two-door station wagon platform, it combined Ford's new-for-'57 car styling with the utility of a pickup by replacing the wagon's covered cargo area with an open bed.

The COE models were extensively revamped for 1957. These C-Series trucks were converted to a forward-control design that placed the steering wheel and pedals ahead of the axle, and the driver seat above it. They were branded "Tilt Cabs" because their cabs tilted forward for engine access.

Major Ford news for '58 was the introduction of the Edsel and a well-received four-passenger evolution of the Thunderbird. Nearly all Ford trucks were restyled to accommodate quad headlights, but the big change—literally—was a new line of large, uprated heavy-duty trucks called Super Duty. These came equipped with new V-8 engines of up to a whopping 534 cubic inches.

For '59, buyers of light-duty trucks could have a factory-built 4×4; previously, Ford trucks had been converted to four-wheel drive by outside manufacturers. Nineteen fifty-nine also brought a redesigned Ranchero, which again echoed the look of the freshly redesigned car line. This would be the last year in which Ranchero would be based on a full-size station wagon chassis.

In 1959, Ford produced its 50-millionth car—a Galaxie hardtop—and outsold Chevy's cars for the year. For 1960, the Big Three jumped into the compact-car fray with Valiant (Chrysler), Corvair (Chevrolet), and Falcon (Ford). The last included a two-door wagon that became the basis for the next-generation Ranchero. Sales of the car/pickup crossover leapt to more than 21,000 for 1960—up from just over 14,000 for 1959.

Falcon would contribute to more good news for trucks in 1961.

1-3. A set-back front axle made the redesigned 1953 F-100 (its name changed from F-1) look nose heavy but allowed for a tighter turning radius. The grille was less ornate this year, and an automatic transmission was available for the first time in the F-100 line.

1. For 1953, heavy-duty F-5 and F-6 Cab-Over-Engine models were replaced by C-500 and C-600 "cab forward" designs. Those were joined, in turn, by larger C-750 (shown) and C-800 variants.

2. At the Dearborn, Michigan, fire station, a converted '52 Ford Sedan Delivery ambulance partnered with a '53 F-700-based fire truck.

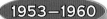

3. Ford's Big Job F-700 and F-750 (shown) had the same 19,500-pound GVW rating, but the former was powered by a six, the latter by a V-8.

4. The T-700 and T-800, a pair of tandem-rear-axle models, were introduced by Ford in 1953. Previously, buyers who wanted a tandem-axle chassis had to have it built using aftermarket parts. The truck seen here is a '54.

1-3. A bigger re-bore brought the six to 223 cubic inches and 115 horsepower for 1954. The star on the grille of this F-100 indicates the six; the hash marks on either side indicate a Deluxe model. The distinctive Ford-truck crest, with lightning bolt and gear cog, had been adopted for 1953.

4. The vertical bumper sections disappeared for 1955 and were replaced by a V-shaped dip in the upper horizontal bar. F-100s now had tubeless tires, and power brakes were a new option.

5. This '55 F-800 Big Job has the factory tandem-axle setup introduced by Ford two years earlier.

1-3. Ford's most popular truck for 1955 was the F-100 with a 6.5-foot bed. By any standard, this was a good-looking vehicle, though Ford still was not giving any special attention to interior cabin design.

4. Because Chevy offered radically modern pickups in 1955, Ford countered with a wrapped windshield and a restyled, carlike dash for 1956. A larger 272-cid V-8 produced 167 horsepower.

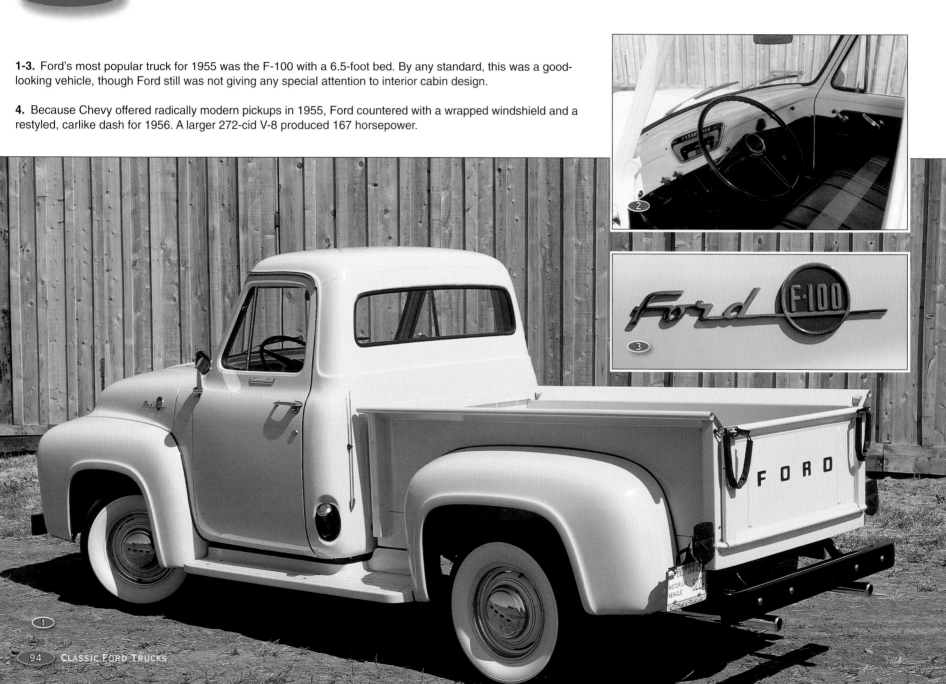

④

1. A dramatic, slab-sided restyle distinguished the 1957 F-Series. The new bed design was called Styleside, though a traditional bed with separate fenders, the Flareside, was still available.

2. The C-Series Tilt Cab forward-control trucks appeared for 1957. They remained on the market with very few visible changes for 34 years. The tilting cab allowed convenient engine access while saving valuable space needed out back for trailers.

3-4. The car-based '57 Ranchero looked like a car with a pickup bed—which is essentially what it was. The stylish, light-duty hauler was a sales sensation despite a starting price of $2098. That was considerably more than the $1789 needed to drive home a Styleside or Flareside F-100. The top Ranchero engine was a 292-cid, 212-horsepower V-8 that wasn't offered in other Ford trucks.

1-2. Ford cars were redesigned for 1959, so Ranchero changed right along with them, picking up two inches in wheelbase and a useful seven inches in cargo-bed length. Interiors also were redesigned.

3. Ford's Extra Heavy Duty line of 1959 offered V-8s displacing up to a whopping 534 cubic inches. Gross Combined Weight (tractor and trailer) climbed to 65,000 pounds with a single rear axle and 75,000 pounds with tandem axles.

4. For 1959, F-250s (shown) and F-350s ordered with automatic transmission came with Ford's new heavy-duty three-speed Cruise-O-Matic. The lighter-duty Fordomatic trans was retained for use in F-100 trucks. F-250 standard beds were 8 feet, but a 7½-foot stake bed was available.

1. Sitting at the top of the F-Series line for '59 were the hood-scooped F-1000 and F-1100 Super Duty trucks. The series was two parallel Super Duty truck lines, one with the COE design and designated C-850, C-950, C-1000, and C-1100; and the other the conventional-cab F-Series, with the same number sequence.

2-3. Except for a change to the grille and the leading edge of the hood, the 1960 F-Series was a carryover. This restored Styleside F-100 runs with a 292-cid V-8 rated at 172 horsepower.

1. Factory-built 4×4s, such as this 1960 F-250, would soon relegate the aftermarket Marmon-Harrington conversions—which had been around since the Thirties—to history.

2. For 1960, Ranchero was no longer based on Ford's full-size line but on the all-new compact Falcon. So, body-on-frame construction was out; unibody was in.

②

CHAPTER 7

1961—1969

The 1960 success of the Falcon-based Ranchero was followed in 1961 by another Falcon derivative, the Econoline Series. Also known as the E-Series, the line included a cargo van, a passenger van, and a pickup truck. The van was almost literally a box on wheels, with the pickup essentially a box with the top rear quarter removed.

1. For 1962, the Falcon-based Ranchero got a new, flush-mounted grille and more aggressive front fenders.

The opposite end of the truck spectrum for '61 was the heavy-duty H-Series, trucks that used modified Ford C-Series Tilt Cabs mounted high on the chassis. The configuration made these modifieds perfect for over-the-road, semi-tractor-trailer duty.

Besides the new releases, Ford introduced a redesigned F-Series line for 1961 that featured new cabs, new front-end sheet metal, and redesigned interiors. They were still offered in traditional Flareside (with separate bed and fenders) and Styleside (smooth-sided bed) versions. But the Styleside was even smoother-sided than before, as the bed was made integral to the cab. Long a feature of the car-based Ranchero, the integrated cab was something new for traditional pickups. However, the integrated cab and bed was offered only on two-wheel-drive models because Ford was concerned about the increased twisting stress that might occur on 4×4s.

Because so much was new for '61, most Ford trucks received only minor updates for '62. Updates and other changes resumed for 1963, when another new series of medium- and heavy-duty models, the N-Series, appeared. Cabs were the same as those used for the F-Series, albeit with significantly shorter noses. This arrangement placed the N-Series between Ford's conventional trucks and the C-Series Tilt Cabs, and made them popular choices for city deliveries and over-the-road semi service where limits on tractor length were enforced.

In other heavy-duty news, Ford expanded diesel offerings to include some F-, C-, and N-Series trucks; previously, only the H-Series offered a diesel engine option.

April 17, 1964, was the debut day for Ford's new Falcon-based Mustang, which would be a tremendous sales hit. On the truck side, 1964 brought a separate box for all Styleside models, rendering the "unibody" pickups artifacts of the past. Also new was a brace of gas engines for the medium- and heavy-duty lines.

Ford's famous Twin I-Beam front suspension made news for 1965. It was exclusive to light-duty 2WD F-Series trucks, bringing a softer ride and better handling characteristics.

Nineteen sixty-six brought a new light-duty truck called Bronco, a sport-utility offered in three body styles, all with either no top or one that could be removed. For the heavy-duty, over-the-road segment, Ford introduced the flat-faced W-Series COE models as replacements for the aging H-Series line. And because Falcon was enlarged in a complete 1966 redesign, the Falcon-based Ranchero grew in size.

Except for extra-heavy-duty models, F-Series trucks were restyled for 1967, and in 1968, medium-size trucks got a diesel engine for the first time. Model-year 1968 also brought a redesign for Ranchero.

Econoline was redesigned for 1969—the first update since its 1961 introduction. The new Econoline was much larger than before and offered an optional V-8 for the first time. The pickup derivative was dropped.

1-2. Besides providing the basis for Ranchero, the Falcon was the foundation of the new Econoline truck series, which included a short, forward-control pickup. The engine sat between the seats beneath a black cover. Shown here is a Deluxe '61, with rear quarter windows and extra chrome trim.

②

1. Econolines were designated E-100, and besides a pickup they were available as vans and as windowed passenger wagons.

2. For 1961, F-100 Styleside pickup beds were integrated with the cabs, but on two-wheel-drive models only; Ford engineers were concerned about excessive torsional flex in 4×4 variants.

3. The P-Series Parcel Delivery established its general look in the early Fifties and hadn't changed appreciably a decade later.

4. Ford introduced the H-Series to its Super Duty line for 1961. The red truck that dominates this ad is a Super Duty conventional, a class that started at the F-750 level.

5. Ford had entered the diesel market in 1961 with Cummins-powered versions of the H-Series high-tilt cab, designated the HD-Series. HD-1000 models (shown) had the largest of those engines, displacing 743 cubic inches and developing 220 horsepower.

BROADER WARRANTIES...GREATER DURABILITY...BIGGER CHOICE !

'61 FORD SUPER DUTY TRUCKS

102 ALL-NEW H-SERIES TILT CAB MODELS—DIESEL AND GAS!

107 C-SERIES TILT CAB MODELS WITH NEW SLEEPER OPTION!

115 NEW HIGH-STRENGTH CONVENTIONAL CAB MODELS!

FORD TRUCKS COST LESS

- New Super Duty V-8 Warranty—100,000 miles or 24 months!
- New extended warranty for entire truck—12 months or 12,000 miles!
- New stronger frames and huskier cabs for Conventional Cab models!
- New 324 money-saving Super Duty models to choose from!

1

1. E-100 pickups (shown) and cargo vans hung on to the Econoline name for 1963, but the wagon was now called "Falcon."

2. F-100 grille changes were always inevitable, and that's what happened for 1963. As before, 4×4 F-Series trucks like the one seen here had a separate cab and bed.

3. Rear-drive F-100s were offered in three bed designs for '63: a separate Styleside, a traditional Flareside (shown), and an integrated Styleside & cab setup. The last would be gone after the 1963 model year.

4. A one-ton payload package was available with '63 Econoline vans.

1. The motor home industry grew dramatically in the Sixties, and to help meet demand, Ford manufactured suitable chassis and powertrains. The grille on this example recalls Ford's then-current N-Series trucks.

2. Twin-I-Beam independent front suspension—two front axles, essentially—brought markedly improved ride comfort to Ford's '65 F-Series.

3. This combined F-100 and Econoline ad from 1964 emphasized Econoline's increased load capacity and optional automatic transmissions—as well as the pickup's longer wheelbase and double-wall cargo bed.

4. The N-Series "short conventional" was new to the Super Duty line for 1963. Note that "DIESEL" appears above the front grille.

1-2. The F-100 picked up two new six-cylinder engines for '65, at 240 and 300 cubic inches, and a new 352-cid V-8. This restored '65 has the V-8, whitewalls, chrome trim, and a two-tone color scheme that's carried over into the cabin.

3. The highest-rated Ford truck for 1965 was the T-950, which rumbled forth with a GVW of up to 78,000 pounds. This one had a Cummins diesel and was designated T-950-D.

4. Bronco made its debut for 1966 as a retort to the Jeep CJ and International Scout. Practical yet sporty, the 4WD Bronco came in three body styles: Wagon (shown), the doorless and topless Roadster, and the Sports Utility.

1. Bronco's Sports Utility was a two-seater with a short pickup bed. Like the Wagon, it had a removable top and a windshield that could be folded flat.

2. A 1967 redesign gave the F-Series a pronounced side spear and a cleaner front-end appearance. And crew cabs (shown) finally got beds that matched the lines of the cab and front fenders.

3. The flat-faced W-Series (shown) replaced the H-Series high-tilt cab in the middle of 1966.

4. In 1966, many of America's tow trucks were F-350s with wrecker bodies.

1. For 1969, the Econoline was redesigned to be much larger than before, making it an attractive choice for family-camper conversion. It also offered a 302-cid V-8 as an optional engine.

2. The engines of '69 Econolines were moved forward; fluids could be checked by lifting the short hood. But now the line had no pickup version, and vans could no longer be ordered with a left-side cargo door.

TurtleTOP
GOSHEN, IND.

① ②

3. As Cadillacs and other large cars fell from favor for ambulance conversion, vans like this E-Series came to the fore.

4. The set-back front axle of the C-Series forward-control truck brought a tight turning radius that made the truck well suited for close-quarters urban work.

①

1970–1982

New government safety regulations took a lot of the air from automobile styling in the Seventies, but because trucks were less in the government's crosshairs, they carried on as dramatically as before—and enjoyed an impressive burst of popularity that's still going strong to this day.

1. The ever-popular F-Series received a facelift for 1976, when a new grille and squarish headlamp bezels appeared. F-150 models were now available in 4WD.

Ford's Kentucky Truck Plant opened in 1970. The facility quickly became known as the Louisville Plant and was notable as the assembly point for the company's L-Series. These heavy-duty trucks replaced the short, conventional N-Series, as well as the bigger F-Series and related tandem-axle T-Series. The Louisville Line thus encompassed a wide range of models serving the medium-, heavy-, and extra-heavy-duty segments and would become one of the most popular truck series Ford ever produced.

Minor trim updates arrived across the board for 1971, and 1972 brought the Courier, a Mazda-built compact pickup with a four-cylinder engine. Courier was intended to compete against the increasingly popular small pickups from Toyota and Datsun.

A redesigned F-Series with longer cabs and restyled exterior body panels arrived for '73—likewise an aerodynamic update of the extra-heavy-duty Cab-Over-Engine W-Series. And Ranchero got a five-mph bumper mandated by the feds for its car-line counterparts.

The OPEC-induced gas crisis of 1973 put everybody on edge, but the F-Series rolled into 1974 with its first extended cab. Econoline grabbed the spotlight for 1975 with its first redesign since growing larger in 1968. But what would turn out to be an even bigger event—though it was hardly that at the time—was the introduction of a "heavy ½-ton" F-Series. Called the F-150, it was created to fill a gap between the F-100 and the F-250. But it turned out to be the first example of what became America's most popular vehicle.

For 1976, Ford decided to cash in on the custom-van craze by offering a factory "custom" Econoline called the Cruising Van. Ford did what a private owner might do: add custom wheels and exterior decoration, and upgrade the interior with plush seats and trim.

Over in the heavy-duty department, Ford offered a new Louisville model, the premium, long-nosed LTL-9000.

In 1977, Ford celebrated its 60th year in the truck business and made hay with the anniversary. Ranchero and Courier were updated, and dress-up packages influenced by the success of the Cruising Van were offered on some other truck lines. And at the close of the 1977 model year, Ford's F-Series pickup was christened the number-one-selling vehicle in the United States.

Bronco enjoyed a major redesign for 1978—the first since its 1966 introduction. Now substantially larger, heavier, and better equipped, the new Bronco was much more popular than its predecessor.

Nineteen seventy-eight also brought a successor to the W-Series extra-heavy-duties, the new CL-9000. More broadly, a successful national sales campaign in support of Ford's 75th Anniversary boosted truck sales.

The now-famous "Built Ford Tough" ad slogan was introduced for 1979, but the year also meant the end of the slumping Ranchero.

The F-Series was restyled for 1980, by which time America was sinking into economic recession. Larger F-Series cabs meant more bang for the buyer's buck, as did independent front suspension—Twin Traction Beam—with four-wheel-drive models. Late in the 1980 model year, medium- and heavy-duty trucks were offered with engines that ran on Liquid Propane (LP) Gas.

An F-100 option for 1981 was a downsized 255-cid V-8 that was even smaller than the standard 300-cid six. Part marketing hype, the 255 nevertheless suggested a fresh Ford commitment to fuel economy.

The Mazda-built Courier compact pickup took its final bow in 1982. The popular F-Series introduced a "FORD" grille oval that replaced the simple "FORD" lettering that had been on the hood's leading edge.

The LTL-9000 continued as the big dog of the company's truck line.

1. Torino was restyled for 1970, and that meant a new look for Ranchero. Base, 500, and GT Ranchero models continued as before; the newest model was the Squire (shown), which wore plenty of simulated wood trim.

Ranchero Squire

429

1-2. Ranger XLT trim was available with some F-Series light trucks for '70, signaling Ford's shift to more luxurious accommodations. Besides wood-grain lift gate appliqué and full-length body moldings, this XLT wears an extra-cost vinyl roof.

3. The LNT-800 was a tandem-axle, short-nose heavy hauler that ran on gasoline. It arrived for 1970 as a replacement for the N-, T-, and largest F-Series models.

4. Ford's light-duty truck family, 1971. Clockwise from left: Bronco sport-ute, a long-wheelbase Econoline Club Wagon, an F-250 Camper Special, and a sporty Ranchero GT.

5. After an 11-year absence, the heavy-duty, gas-powered VC-900 version of the Tilt Cab returned to the Ford truck lineup.

1. The Bronco sport-utility was fitted with a heavy-duty axle for 1971. Interior comfort was heightened by newly standard front bucket seats.

2. Four-wheel-drive F-250s got a beefier Spicer front axle for 1972.

3. An F-250 Camper Special was offered on the crew cab chassis-and-cab platform for '72.

4. This 1971 LTS was fitted for tanker duty. The setback front axle allowed the cab to carry a greater percentage of the total load.

1-3. For '72, Broncos with the Sport option package had bright trim inside and out, plus fancier upholstery. All Broncos got bigger brakes that year. The spare snugged between the rear seatback and liftgate.

4. Clockwise from top left, Ford's domestically made light trucks for 1973: Bronco, F-100, and Ranchero. The last got a front-end facelift, and the F-100 picked up an all-new cab design and front sheet metal.

5. Limited-edition Explorer pickups that returned for 1973 included lower-body striping.

①

1. Dodge pioneered extended-cab pickups in 1973, and Ford responded in '74 with its SuperCab model with an optional forward-facing bench or side-facing jump seats.

2. What's a good way to haul a cement mixer? With a heavy-duty, diesel-powered LTS-9000 platform.

3. The third generation of Econoline vans and wagons arrived for '75. Wheelbases were extended to 124 and 138 inches, and GVW rose across the board. An all-new model was called the E-150.

4. The F-150 joined the F-Series for 1975. The 150 split the difference in payload capacity between the F-100 and F-250, and became hugely popular.

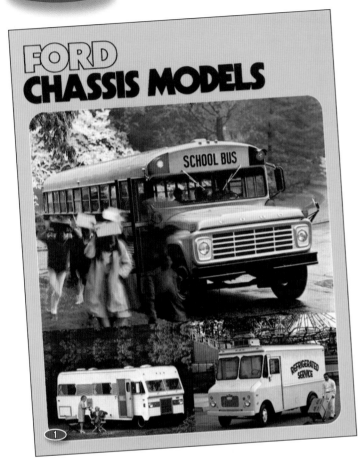

FORD
CHASSIS MODELS

1. This commercial-chassis brochure from 1976 offers school bus platforms in a choice of six wheelbase lengths.

2. The Mazda-built Courier pickup was restyled for 1977. A new, second model had a seven-foot cargo bed.

3. The L-Series's LTL-9000 ran with a Cummins NTC-350 diesel and a 10-speed Fuller Roadranger transmission.

4. An accessorized '77 F-100 "Shorty Flareside" with 4WD.

1

2

1. A new, 104-inch-wheelbase Bronco was derived from F-Series trucks for the '78 model year. A 351-cid V-8 was standard, with a 400-cid unit available.

2. Ford's topline COE hauler for 1978 was the CLT-9000. The aerodynamic aluminum CL cab could be ordered with air springs that smoothed out road shocks.

3. Newly positioned at the top of the F-Series light-duty line for 1978 was the plush Ranger Lariat.

3

1. America's van craze is suggested by this factory-embellished 1980 Econoline, which had portholes, tape stripes, and fancy wheels. Interiors were even more detailed and kitted out for maximum style and comfort. Suddenly, you were "vanning."

2. For 1980, Ford redesigned its medium-duty trucks to more closely resemble the company's heavy-duty Louisville line. This one runs with a 370-cubic-inch V-8 (with 4-barrel carburetor), the smallest of the so-called Ford 385 engines that were named for a 3.85-inch crankshaft stroke. The 370 was exclusive to the medium trucks; other displacements in the 385 series were 429, 460, and 514 cubic inches.

3. The tradition of annual styling updates to the F-Series ended in 1979, when that year's trucks were virtually identical to the '78 models. The F-150 was by now the best-selling truck in America, and Ford reasoned that there was no need to mess with success.

4. Ford's light trucks could be had with a variety of custom decor packages for 1980. These included blackout grille, aluminum or white-painted wheels, two-tone paint, and tape stripes.

①

Classic   Hi Liner   Free Spirit

1. For 1982, F-Series trucks added the blue Ford oval to the middle of their grilles and killed the "Ford" letters that had adorned the leading edge of the hood. In a nod to fuel economy, the F-100 came standard with a new 232-cid V-6. Pictured is an F-150.

2. This Ford brochure art from 1982 shows off the big dogs of the truck line, the LTLs, which were exclusively diesel powered. Engines were by Cummins, Caterpillar, and Detroit Diesel. Horsepower ratings ranged from 300 to 445.

CHAPTER 9
1983–1990

The slow-selling Mazda-built Courier was replaced for 1983 with the Ford-built Ranger, which quickly became the best-selling compact pickup in America. Confirmation of the new truck's popularity came in 1984, when the Ranger-based Bronco II sport-ute was added to the lineup. Both the Ranger and the Bronco II carried styling cues that linked them to their F-Series and Bronco big brothers.

1. This 1987 F-350 with crew cab seated three in back, which made the truck appealing not just to work crews but to families. Optional on the truck this year was a 6.9-liter International Harvester diesel.

①

Another piece of noteworthy news for '84 was the discontinuation of the F-100, a model name that had been around since 1953. The truck's gross vehicle weight fell below the threshold that would have allowed it to get by on the less-stringent emissions standards that applied to heavier-duty trucks. But the demise of the F-100 was more of a historical loss than a sales one, as the slightly beefier F-150, which had been introduced in 1975, absorbed those buyers and gained many more besides.

Fuel injection arrived for 1985 but on selected engines only: the 5.0-liter (302 cid) V-8 in F-Series and Bronco, and the 2.3-liter four in the Ranger. More engines adopted the system over the next few years, and all Ford truck motors were fuel injected by the end of the decade.

In response to the surprisingly popular Dodge Caravan and Plymouth Voyager minivans introduced by Chrysler Corporation in 1984, Ford brought out the Aerostar van for 1986. Because it was built on a rear-wheel-drive truck frame, the Aerostar was closer to a traditional van than to the front-drive/unibody Chryslers, and that—along with its available V-6—gave it a higher towing capacity.

The year also brought a new name to Ford's medium-duty lineup: the Cargo. Unusual in that it carried a name instead of a series designation, the Cargo was described as a "low tilt cab," though the cab was in fact rather tall. Designed around European styling themes, Cargo was intended to replace the boxy, Fifties-vintage C-Series Tilt Cab—still in production—but the two were sold side by side through the end of the decade. Finally, 1986 brought a SuperCab version of the Ranger pickup.

For 1987, Ford's light-duty F-Series trucks and their full-size Bronco counterparts were treated to a long-awaited restyle that brought aerodynamic design touches to the front ends. They also picked up rear-wheel antilock brakes, as did the smaller Bronco II. And unhappy news came from Ford's executive suite in 1987: Henry Ford II, who had been instrumental in "saving" Ford Motor in the late Forties and was a key figure in the corporation until 1982, died of pneumonia at the age of 70.

A new line of Super Duty F-350 trucks was introduced for the 1988 model year. These filled a gap between the regular F-350s and the medium-duty F-600s. A 7.5-liter V-8 was standard while a 7.3L diesel was optional. F-Series dropped its available Flareside bed this year, though the box would return a few years later.

Bigger news for 1988—literally—was the debut of a sleek new Class 8 truck called AeroMax. Although the cab was similar to that used for its L-Series Louisville stablemates, the front end was given an aero look and the interior was more refined.

For 1989, Bronco II and Ranger were redesigned for the first time since their introductions, getting aerodynamically sleeker front ends. Ranger also picked up rear-wheel antilock brakes as standard. The Aerostar minivan added a "midi" version with a longer body.

Ford announced that the beloved medium-duty C-Series Tilt Cab, which had been introduced for 1957 and soldiered on for more than 30 years with hardly a change or complaint, was to be decommissioned. The truck was popular to the end.

Ford's truck division entered the Nineties in fine shape: The F-150 was the best-selling vehicle in the nation, the Ranger made its mark as the best-selling compact pickup, and larger Ford trucks competed effectively in their respective market segments.

1. Model-year 1982 was the last for the Mazda-built Courier compact pickup. It was replaced for '83 with the Ford-built Ranger (shown). Unlike the Courier, Ranger could be had with not only a gas-powered four, but with a diesel four or a gas V-6.

1

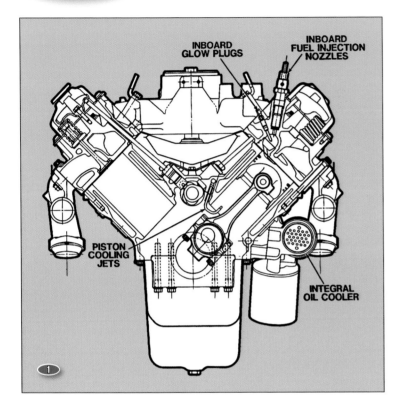

1. For 1983, Ford's 6.9-liter diesel V-8 was optional on the F-250 Heavy Duty and the F-350.

2. The '83 F-350 was the only F-Series pickup available as a four-door, six-passenger crew cab.

3. The '83 F-Series medium-duty line added three trucks with GVW ratings that pushed them nearly into heavy-duty territory: the tandem-axle FT-800 and FT-900, and the FT-8000 diesel (shown).

4. The 1979 gasoline crisis prompted Detroit to think about fuel economy and smaller vehicles. The '84 Bronco II, then, was at the vanguard of a whole new segment: the compact sport-ute. At the wheelbase, it was 10 inches shorter than the full-size Bronco and 19 inches shorter overall.

5. Bronco II was based on the compact Ranger pickup and weighed more than 800 pounds less than its Bronco big brother. All Bronco IIs were 4WD and ran with a 2.8-liter V-6. A bold XLS package added tri-color tape stripes.

1

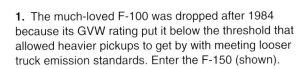

Dear New Truck Buyer:

Quality is Job 1 at Ford Motor Company. This isn't just a phrase. It's a commitment to total quality.

Total quality begins with the design and engineering of our trucks and continues through the life of the product. We plan them with a vision of the customer—of you—sitting behind the wheel of a new truck.

Total quality will be apparent to you through functional performance, overall vehicle integrity, the "look and feel" of materials, satisfying aesthetics, safety, serviceability and cost of ownership.

Total quality requires continuous improvement in everything we do. Every employee at Ford Motor Company is involved in the process of meeting your needs and expectations.

I invite you to look over our new 1985 Ford trucks in your dealer's showroom. Test drive them on the road. When you do, I think you'll understand all that's involved in the total quality concept at Ford Motor Company.

Donald E. Petersen
President
Ford Motor Company

1. The much-loved F-100 was dropped after 1984 because its GVW rating put it below the threshold that allowed heavier pickups to get by with meeting looser truck emission standards. Enter the F-150 (shown).

2. Via form letter, Ford Motor president Donald E. Petersen advised truck buyers that the bywords for 1985 would be "Quality is Job 1."

3. For '85, F-Series trucks got a newly optional fuel-injected 5.0-liter V-8.

4. Ford's response to Chrysler's successful minivans was the Aerostar, which came with a 2.3-liter four or an optional 2.8-liter V-6.

1. Ranger's new-for-'86 SuperCab added 17 inches of passenger room but was available with the six-foot bed only. Regular cabs had an optional seven-foot bed.

2. Ranger's off-road High Rider package arrived for 1987 with a bed-mounted light bar and a tubular grille guard.

(3)

1983–1990

3. Model-year 1987 brought Bronco the same front-end and interior restyle as the F-Series pickups, plus standard rear-wheel anti-lock brakes and a fuel-injected six.

4. The F-Series's first major update since 1980 showed up for 1987. The new look was more aerodynamic than before, with rounded front corners and flush-mounted headlights. Interiors were also redesigned.

(4)

1. Ford's medium-duty line for 1987, represented by (from left), an L-8000 with set-back front axle, a COE Cargo, and an F-Series.

2. Ford built its own turbocharged diesel engines in 1987 and installed them in its medium-duty trucks. The powerplants' horsepower ratings ranged from 160 to 240.

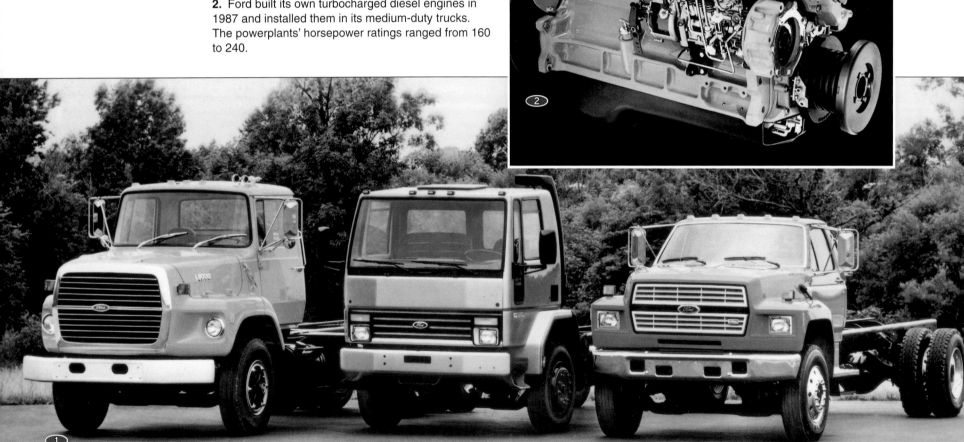

3-4. The LTL-9000 was Ford's Class-8 conventional. Improved Cummins and Caterpillar diesel engines provided as much as 400 horsepower. A revised cabin and dash arrived for 1987; the dash seen here has extra instrumentation.

1983–1990

1

1. Bronco was carried into 1988 with few visible changes—but underhood, all engines were now fuel injected.

2. A CLT Cab-Over-Engine (COE) Class 8 made a promotional tour of the United States in 1987.

3. Ford dropped its retro Flareside pickup bed for 1988, so all pickups had the flush Styleside design, as seen on this F-150.

4. The L-7000 was a lighter-duty version of the heavy-duty L-Series line that effectively fell into the medium-duty segment. The top L-Series truck was the 9000.

1

1. Ranger got a sleek new front end for 1989.

2. Bronco II shared Ranger's front-end restyle for '89.

3. This corporate photo confirms how very little the COE C-Series had changed from its 1957 debut (right) to its final iteration in 1990 (left).

4. Aerostar received a mildly freshened front end for 1989 and a new, extended-length version.

①

CHAPTER 10

1991–2002

Toward the end of the 1990 model year, Ford released a new sport-utility called the Explorer. Available in two- and four-door form, it was designated a 1991 model and quickly became the best-selling SUV in the U.S. So enormous was (and is) this success that it's difficult to overstate the importance of Explorer to Ford and its influence on the larger automotive industry.

1. While it made hay with the new Explorer, Ford brought back the high-performance F-150 Lightning (shown) for 1999 after a three-year hiatus. The truck had an exclusive supercharged version of the 5.4-liter V-8 pushing out a mighty 360 horsepower.

To make room for Explorer, however, Bronco II, whose tidy size and reasonable fuel efficiency encouraged a devoted following, was killed.

Ford celebrated 75 years in the truck business in 1992, a year that brought a redesign of the full-size Econoline vans—a welcome modernization, as these vehicles hadn't seen major changes since 1975.

The 1993 model year brought a similar update of the Ranger compact pickup, and the debut of a high-performance F-150 called the Lightning. Ford's Special Vehicle Team (SVT) built it for buyers who wanted the utility of a pickup with the power and handling of a performance car.

Safety was emphasized again for '94, when the Econoline picked up four-wheel antilock brakes and the F-Series got a driver-side airbag.

A front-wheel-drive minivan called Windstar arrived for 1995, and although it was intended to replace the aging Aerostar, the continuing popularity of the latter meant that Windstar would have an older stablemate until the Aerostar was finally retired after 1997.

Besides a freshened appearance for 1995, the Explorer picked up a flexible-fuel version (FFV) that could run on a mixture of gasoline and corn-based ethanol. In 1996, Mercury dealers were handed their own version of the Explorer, dubbed Mountaineer.

The big Class 7 and 8 Louisville line models, and the Class 8 AeroMax trucks, were totally redesigned for 1996 at considerable cost in R&D, time, and money. The changes situated these fine trucks for entry into the 21st Century. Imagine public surprise, then, when Ford sold these lines to archrival Freightliner, so that valuable production space could be freed up for Ford's highly profitable light-duty trucks, such as Explorer and the F-150.

Model-year 1997 brought the most radical changes yet seen to the popular F-Series. Because the rollout began in calendar-year 1996, only the new F-150s were initially available, and were sold alongside 1996 models. Rollouts eventually encompassed heavy-duty pickups, such as the F-250 HD and the F-350. The redesigned F-Series won *Motor Trend*'s Truck of the Year Award.

After a long run, the full-size, two-door Bronco SUV came to the end of the road, and in its place came the even larger Expedition, which was based on the aforementioned new 1997 F-Series.

In 1998, Ford celebrated the 50th Anniversary of its F-series brand with burgeoning sales. At the compact end of the scale, Ranger was fitted with a longer cab and larger standard engine, along with an electric-powered model. And Lincoln dealers got the Navigator, an upscale version of the Expedition.

For 2000, the Expedition/Navigator seemed shrunken next to the new Excursion, a super-sized sport-ute that was larger than anything else on the market. Because it rode the F-250 Super Duty chassis, the Excursion outweighed its closest rival, the Chevy Suburban, by nearly a ton! Early buyers liked the towing capacity and cavernous interior.

Ford partnered with Harley-Davidson in 2000 to produce the Harley-Davidson F-150, which was essentially an aggressive trim package.

For '01, the compact Escape sport-utility was available with a four or a six. The same model year brought the Explorer Sport Trac, a crew-cab pickup with an open rear bed instead of an enclosed cargo area.

The F-150 got a crew cab for '01 called the SuperCrew, and Ranger picked up a sporty enclosed version called the Edge. And anybody who wanted to tow large, fifth-wheel trailers in style could buy a decked-out four-door F-650 called the Super CrewZer.

Explorer was completely redesigned for 2002, the first major alteration since its 1991 introduction. A third-row seating option and standard independent rear suspension were among the new features.

1. The Ford Explorer was introduced in the spring of 1990 as a '91 model and immediately gobbled up the competition. A major and enduring success, Explorer was similar to the Bronco II but offered a four-door version as well as a two-door. The '91 shared Ranger's 155-hp 4.0-liter V-6 and could tow 5500 pounds.

2. The Nite was a new F-150 trim package for '91, highlighted by blackout trim.

1. F-Series pickups were given restyled front ends for 1992, and the Flareside bed returned after a four-year absence. It was available on regular and extended-cab models.

2. "Cherry-picker" duty is handled by this '91 F-800. The grille badge reveals that the truck is powered by Ford's 429-cid four-barrel V-8.

3. The Ecostar was an experimental electric vehicle that, although not sold to the general public, saw some use as a fleet vehicle. It was based on Ford of Europe's Escort Van and claimed that its sodium-sulfur battery pack provided a top speed of 75 mph and a range of 100 miles.

4. Although Ranger got a front-end re-do for 1993, powertrains carried over.

④

1. The F-150 Nite appearance package went away for 1993 and was replaced with the performance-oriented Lightning running with a special 240-horse version of the 5.8-liter V-8.

2. Besides a revised grille, the 1995 Ranger could be had with a driver-side airbag and four-wheel antilock brakes. The base 2.3-liter four gained 4 horsepower, to 112.

3. The all-new, front-drive Windstar van (shown) was intended to replace Aerostar for '95, but the latter kept its popularity long enough that the two vans were sold side by side for a few seasons. Windstar had V-6 engines of 3.0 and 3.8 liters.

4. Four years old in 1995, Explorer received its first styling changes: a new grille, rounded front end, and a revised interior with dual front airbags.

1. A sloped windshield and rounded front contours were the main cosmetic changes to the big Louisville line for 1996. This example has a set-back front axle.

2. Ford's top truck line for '96 was the new AeroMax 9500. Its raked windshield and rounded edges contributed to a generally slippery nature.

3. The redesigned 1996 Louisville truck line included models without a set-back front axle. Thus configured, the trucks had much flatter front ends.

③

①

1. The 1997 F-Series wore its most significant restyle since 1980. Early production focused on F-150 SuperCab versions, which featured a rear-hinged back door on the passenger side. These half-doors could be opened only after the corresponding front door was opened. Shown here is a regular-cab version.

2. The 1998 Electric Ranger had conventional lead-acid batteries mounted between the frame rails and a rear-mounted 90-horsepower electric motor. Ford claimed a 75-mph top speed and a 35-50-mile range. Power-sucking air conditioning was optional.

3. The four-door Expedition effectively replaced the two-door Bronco as Ford's full-size SUV for 1997. Expedition was based on the F-150, giving it an impeccable, and popular, pedigree. A third-row seat that allowed for nine-passenger capacity was a well-liked option.

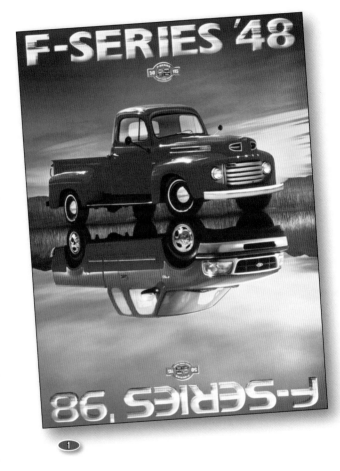

1

2

3

1. Ford celebrated the F-Series's 50th Anniversary with promotions that included this clever inverted poster. The milestone was a significant one in automotive history.

2. Many Ford fans were dismayed when the company sold its heavy-duty truck lines to Freightliner in the late Nineties, in order to concentrate on its hugely popular light- and medium-duty trucks. Shown is one of the last Ford-built Louisville-line trucks, versions of which would later be badged as Sterlings.

3. Ranger's '98 extended Super-Cab offered dual rear-hinged back doors, a feature not available on any other contemporary compact pickup.

4. After Ford sold the tooling for its AeroMax and Louisville models to Freightliner, the L-750 (shown) became the biggest Ford truck. This is a 1999 model.

1. The 2000 F-150 Harley-Davidson pickup was a licensing arrangement that picked up Harley identifiers. It was available only in black and only in SuperCab form. Power came from a 260-hp 5.4-liter V-8.

2. The uber-large Excursion sport utility arrived for 2000. It was based on the F-250 Super Duty pickup and was cheerfully advertised as the world's largest and heaviest sport-ute. Everybody came to their senses after the 2005 model year, when Excursion was discontinued.

3. For 2001, the F-150 became the first ½-ton pickup to offer four conventional side doors (on SuperCrew crew-cab models).

4. The 2001 Escape compact SUV was a joint venture with Mazda.

1-2. The F-650 Super CrewZer was new for 2001. It had a luxury interior and a turbo-diesel that produced 300 horsepower.

3. A redesigned Explorer was introduced as an early 2002 model. Ford's very popular sport-ute now had a roomier interior, available third-row seating, and class-exclusive independent rear suspension.

①

CHAPTER 11

2003–2012

A 2003 event held in Dearborn, Michigan, celebrated the 100th Anniversary of the Ford Motor Company—an enormous milestone for a company founded on the talent and drive of a single man. To commemorate the event, Ford issued special Heritage Edition F-150s with two-tone paint and interior treatments, along with "1903–2003" Heritage Edition badges.

1. Ranger, Ford's compact pickup, was redesigned for 2006, bringing it in line visually with the rest of the company's truck line. The cockpit and dash became more modern and carlike, too.

Other specially trimmed pickups were released for 2003: the Harley-Davidson F-150 with "100th Anniversary Edition" badges and available black-over-silver paint; and the King Ranch F-150 with rich leather upholstery and other unique features.

For 2004, some carryover '03 F-150s were registered as 2004 models and sold in regular-cab and SuperCab form as the F-150 Heritage. The Heritage vanished after 2004, having existed in the first place only so that production on true '04 trucks could have time to ramp up.

Significant changes were seen on true 2004 F-150s that were completely redesigned inside and out, and rode a new chassis. Regular-cab versions now had narrow, rear-hinged "quarter doors" in back that were similar to the SuperCab's "half doors." Also, a new SuperCrew offered four conventional doors.

New for 2005 was a gas/electric hybrid version of the Escape compact SUV. Its drivetrain coupled a gas-sipping four-cylinder engine with an electric motor.

Also new this year was a car-based crossover SUV called Freestyle. Larger than the Escape and less trucklike than the Explorer, the Freestyle could seat up to seven and featured Ford's first Continuously Variable Transmission (CVT).

A revised version of the very popular Explorer was introduced for 2006, with bolder styling, a redesigned interior, and an updated chassis. A more powerful V-8 was offered, too, mated to a new six-speed automatic transmission.

For '07, Expedition's redesign picked up more F-Series cues and offered an EL version with an added 14.8 inches of usable length. And the new Explorer Sport Trac came on the scene with a fresh V-8 rated at 292 horsepower.

Significant news came from the big Super Duty line, which added an F-450, with a payload rating of more than three tons and capable of towing better than 24,000 pounds. The truck's new 6.4-liter Power Stroke diesel helped.

The hot-selling F-150 was updated for 2009, with a lighter but stronger steel frame; standard Roll Stability Control and Trailer Sway Control; improved front and rear suspensions; and a larger interior.

Twenty-ten brought the Transit Connect, a four-cylinder box van with optional side and rear windows. Oh, and it was made in Turkey.

The year also introduced the F-150 Raptor, another offering from Ford's Special Vehicles Team (SVT). With shock and braking biases altered from stock, Raptor could travel rutted roads at speeds that would destroy other light trucks. An all-new 6.2-liter V-8 rated at 400 horsepower provided the power.

A glimpse of the future rode in for 2011 with the electric Transit Connect, which ran with a 28-kwh lithium battery pack. Range was about 75 miles, and a full recharge could be accomplished at a standard 240-volt outlet in six to eight hours.

Explorer got the re-do treatment for 2011, with fresh emphasis on the "crossover" part of its appeal. Now of unibody construction, Explorer offered its most carlike ride yet and sufficient oomph from its 3.5-liter V-6 and smooth six-speed automatic transmission. Some towing capacity was lost, but Explorer was now a better-balanced vehicle, equipped to go against GMC's Acadia, Toyota's Highlander, and similar SUVs.

For 2012, Edge enjoyed a major freshening with revised styling and a new interior, plus a new 3.5-liter V-6 producing 265 horsepower. Vehicles like Edge now accounted for an important share of Ford's truck business.

Twenty-twelve also brought a fresh Harley-Davidson F-150 and, for the F-250 Super Duty, a 400-horse turbo diesel. Elsewhere in the line, a new 3.5-liter EcoBoost V-6 was introduced.

Finally, the perennially popular Ranger, now for export only, was redesigned for '12 on a compact-truck platform developed by Ford of Australia.

1

1. The popular Expedition was redesigned for 2003, picking up the industry's first power-folding third-row seat, plus independent rear suspension and available antiskid control and curtain side airbags.

2. The look of Ford's minivan was updated for 2004, and the vehicle's name was changed, too, from Windstar to Freestar. A variant was sold at Mercury dealers as the Monterey. Top engine was a new 201-horsepower 4.2-liter V-6.

2

2003–2012

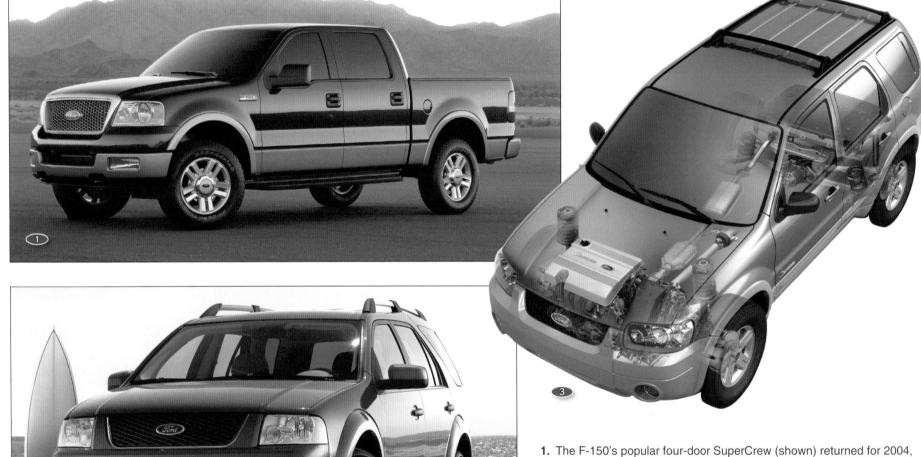

1. The F-150's popular four-door SuperCrew (shown) returned for 2004, but all body styles now had four doors—even the regular cab, with two small "quarter doors" in back.

2. Ford's '05 Freestyle crossover could be had in front- or all-wheel drive.

3. The 2005 Escape Hybrid ran with a 2.3-liter gasoline, four-cylinder engine and battery-powered electric motor mated to Ford's first continuously variable automatic transmission.

4. In its swan-song year as an '05 model, the enormous Excursion was given a fresh face that couldn't obscure the pressure of increasingly higher gas prices that helped doom the vehicle.

5. Middleweight F-450 and F-550 Super Duty trucks were redesigned for 2005 with Ford's familiar "nostril" truck grille.

6. Econoline vans continued to be popular conversion vehicles in '06. Versatile and hardy, they were tabbed by commercial users ranging from tour operators to general contractors. The Econoline-based bus seen here ran with an experimental hydrogen-powered V-10.

1. The sport-utility market was becoming crowded in 2006, but Ford maintained Explorer's top-dog status with a comprehensive makeover.

2. Changes to Explorer for '06 included a reengineered inner structure, a revised suspension, and an available 292-horsepower V-8.

3. The redone 2006 Explorer interior was practical and carlike, with well-placed gauges and most controls in easy reach.

4

4. The 2007 Edge was Ford's new car-based midsize SUV. It was a five-passenger wagon that shared a platform with the Ford Fusion. Power came from a 265-hp V-6.

5. The Sport Trac—an Explorer with an open, four-by-five foot cargo bed—was redesigned for '07 and picked up an independent rear suspension and an available V-8, too.

5

①

1. Expedition, by now Ford's largest SUV, was restyled front and rear for 2007 and offered an extended-wheelbase model called the EL. This one tows a rival Chevy Tahoe.

2. Ford's heavy-duty F-650 (shown) and F-750 were chassis-cab trucks ready to be outfitted to suit the needs of businesses and municipalities. The top engine choice was a 7.2-liter Caterpillar inline six producing 300 horses and 860 pound-feet of torque.

②

3. Beefier F-Series trucks offered several new trim options for '07, such as this Outlaw package for the F-250 Super Duty Lariat crew cab. Goodies included front captain's chairs, console, color-keyed bumper and grille, chrome tubular side steps, chrome exhaust tips, and unique trim inside and out.

1

1-2. Flex, a new mid-size SUV that seated six or seven, came in four trim levels: base, SE, midlevel SEL, and top-line Limited (shown). SEL and Limited had available all-wheel drive. Engine/transmission combo was a 262-horsepower 3.5-liter V-6 mated to a six-speed automatic.

2

3. A substantial 2009 update brought the F-150 more power and increased passenger room. The base V-6 was gone, replaced with a 248-horsepower 4.6-liter V-8.

4. The F-150 Platinum was added for 2009 to fill the gap left by the departed F-150-based Lincoln Mark LT. This luxo-truck had a fine-mesh grille; 20-inch, 16-spoke alloy wheels; and interior wood, brushed aluminum, and specific leather trim.

1. Edge gained a dressy Limited version for 2008 and a Sport model (shown) for '09. Sport had unique body panels, standard 22-inch wheels, and dual exhausts.

2. The Transit Connect van was assembled for Ford in Turkey and came to the U.S. as a 2010 model. It seated between two and five, and could be configured with various combinations of glass windows and steel panels.

3. The rugged F-650/F-750 chassis came in a variety of cab types.

④

⑤

⑥

4. For 2011, Ford's F-150 pickups were available as base XL, sporty STX, off-road FX-4, volume XLT, uplevel King Ranch and Lariat, and top-line Platinum (shown).

5. Lincoln's big Navigator SUV was based on the Ford Expedition and was positioned in the marketplace against Cadillac's popular Escalade.

6. An EcoBoost 3.5-liter V-6 was a new addition to the 2011 F-150 line. It produced 365 horsepower and 420 pound-feet of torque.

1. The venerable Econoline celebrated its 40th anniversary in 2011, its popularity as a full-size van undiminished.

2. Like the related Ford Edge, Lincoln's MKX crossover was heavily revised for '11. More power—from a new 305-hp 3.7-liter V-6—was a solid selling point.

3. The big change for the 2011 Explorer was a switch from body-on-frame construction to crossover-style unibody design. Front- and AWD versions were available.

4. The 6.7-liter Power Stroke V-8 that helped move this 2012 F-250 Super Duty was a turbo-diesel unit developing 400 horsepower and 800 pound-feet of torque. The compacted graphite iron block was stronger than cast iron.

5. The 7-passenger 2012 Flex had the only available refrigerated console in its class. Engine choices were a 3.5-liter, 262-horsepower V-6 or a 3.5-liter EcoBoost six rated at 355 horses.

6. The 2012 Harley-Davidson F-150 came standard with a 6.2-liter gasoline-powered V-8 that made 411 horsepower and 434 pound-feet of torque. Trailer towing capacity was 7500 pounds. The truck had 22-inch machined-aluminum wheels, snakeskin-leather interior accents, and snakeskin-texture bodyside graphics.

1. Buyers of a 2012 Lincoln MKT chose between a 3.7-liter Duratec V-6 and a 3.5-liter Ecoboost V-6. Horsepower was 268 and 355, respectively. The EcoBoost came standard on the AWD model.

2. For 2012, anti-rollover technology was standard on the Transit Connect. Maximum payload capacity was 1600 pounds, and cargo space topped out at 129.6 cubic inches. Rear side doors slid fore and aft; back doors swung open to 180 degrees, with a 255-degree span optional.

3. Riding a platform developed by Ford's Australian operations, the redesigned export-only 2012 Ranger had best-in-class water-wading capacity of 31.5 inches with a full load. A waterproof fuel tank and raised electricals helped make it possible.